Finding God in the Quantum

To Darlene,
with great appreciation
for your lovely spirit and
friendship.

Warm regards,
John
1/28/?

Finding God in the Quantum

◆

A Spirituality of Oneness

Dr. John L. Walker

iUniverse, Inc.
New York Lincoln Shanghai

Finding God in the Quantum
A Spirituality of Oneness

iUniverse books may be ordered through booksellers or by contacting:

iUniverse
2021 Pine Lake Road, Suite 100
Lincoln, NE 68512
www.iuniverse.com
1-800-Authors (1-800-288-4677)

ISBN-13: 978-0-595-39985-7 (pbk)
ISBN-13: 978-0-595-84373-2 (ebk)
ISBN-10: 0-595-39985-1 (pbk)
ISBN-10: 0-595-84373-5 (ebk)

Printed in the United States of America

To my wonderful wife Corky, my constant inspiration.

Contents

Preface

by
The Reverend Geofrey G. Layng

Are you ready for a revelation of Truth? Are you open to an expanded consciousness about yourself and God? It is all here in this book by Dr. John Walker, who understands the relationship of science and theology. You are in for a treat! John explains, in simple terms, how particle and wave consciousness work together to create our Infinite Consciousness.

He explains how we are all commingled with everything throughout the physical universe. This book is for those who seek to know why things happen in our lives and how to change ineffective experiences into profound events. If you are even a little bit curious about unraveling the "mysteries" of life, this book will astound you. You will be released from a localized belief in yourself to a revelation of infinite wholeness.

This book reminds me of the time that Edgar Mitchell called me and told me of his defining experience as an astronaut on the moon in 1971. When he viewed the Earth he said: "I saw this huge blue planet swimming in a sea of electromagnetic energy. I had a spontaneous alteration of consciousness. I knew instantly that there was inclusive life throughout the universe." Similarly, after reading this book you will have a spontaneous change of consciousness. You will never go back to your old way of thinking. This book will expand your perception of reality from four dimensions to your inclusive Infinite Dimension of Reality. I bless all who read these principles of truth and apply them in their lives.

(Rev. Layng is a physicist, minister and a professional speaker. His favorite talks are on quantum science and how philosophy, theology, and science are creating our new spiritual dimensions of reality.)

Introduction

What is the true nature of God?

The bewildering variety of religious movements, churches, sects, and belief groups around the world indicates two things to me: 1) humankind in general is searching for a true relationship with God; 2) few people have found it yet.

I am not concerned by all the existing individualized paths toward spirituality because individuality can easily live in the Oneness that is God. Each person ultimately has to follow his or her own path, and individuality can lead to great achievement. What does concern me is that there is no basic underlying unity to all the religious searching that is happening now and has been happening throughout history. In fact, I not only see a lack of increase in spiritual awareness even as civilization in general is increasing in other areas at a breakneck pace, but I see steps backward toward savagery in the continuing antagonisms and wars based on differing religious viewpoints based on descriptions from long ago.

I think that it is time for a change. I feel that a proper and true understanding of God would be universal enough to end religious bickering from differences of beliefs so that a reality of oneness could express itself among people, yet could still allow each person to develop his or her own spirituality with the support of all others. I think that recent advances of knowledge in physics and in levels of consciousness can lead us all to such an understanding within the realm of faith, and I feel that such an increase in awareness is a step for all of humanity whose time has come.

The purposes of this little book are: to indicate a truer perception of God than some of us may now have; to suggest ways in which we can use this perception to recognize our oneness within diversity; and to help us set plans to actually achieve peace and enlightenment in our present lives. It asks us to step away from our specialized thinking momentarily to gain a new spiritual awareness by looking at some universal ideas and observations outside of our established religious struc-

Finding God in the Quantum

tures, and then incorporate them through our own prayers, contemplations, imaging, and actions to receive our own intuitions of truth from God.

I feel that such universal ideas and concepts can help humanity and all of creation grow in enlightenment and therefore find the beauty, peace, happiness, and fulfillment that true spirituality can bring. Let us start to use them by Finding God in the Quantum.

PART I
The Awareness

Deciphering the Three Pillars

How can Robin Hood, George Washington, Sherlock Holmes, and Galileo Galilei start us off on a pursuit of the true nature of God?

Robin Hood, famous in legend, and George Washington, famous as the first president of the United States, both met their mortal ends when they fell sick and the doctors of the day treated them in the only way they knew: letting a quantity of blood to get rid of the toxins. They let too much. This old-time style of treatment cannot hold a candle to today's sophisticated practice of medicine with its vastly expanded awareness of the complexities of the body and of the astonishing variety of ways to heal it.

The fictional detective Sherlock Holmes solved his cases using careful observation of such things as cigar ash residue (he could identify 140 different kinds) or people's hands (he wrote a monograph on the hands of slaters, sailors, cork-cutters, compositors, weavers, and diamond polishers). It is obvious that modern detective work using such methods as fingerprints, infra-red and ultra-violet photography, and DNA analysis has made tremendous advancements since Sherlock's day.

Galileo with his telescope confirmed the view of Copernicus that the earth was not the center of the universe, but he barely escaped the wrath of the church authorities for his declarations, spending his last years under house arrest. Of course, the great advances in astronomy and knowledge of the earth since then leave the views of the church in his day completely void.

Yet it seems that great numbers of people still try to understand God using the simple knowledge and understandings of authors who were writing hundreds or even thousands of years ago as if no advances in theology had been made since then. The ancient writers of the books of the Bible, for instance, were accustomed to a world of tribal chiefs or kings on thrones, and they depicted God accordingly since that was the type of ruler they could understand. Such chiefs had human

3

failings; required strict methods of service and adoration by their subjects; needed help in fighting battles against powerful enemies; were capricious and unpredictable; dealt with people through judgment, punishment, force, and fear; and were partial to some while hostile to others. It is not surprising that ancients pictured God in these ways.

To be blunt, then, we should not be surprised when terrorists are willing to kill men, women, and even innocent children indiscriminately in an effort to cleanse a land of people professing different religious beliefs from theirs when we see the God of the Old Testament directing that very effort through Joshua, as just one example. It is hard to see a God of peace and love for all people in this interpretation of history. Perhaps a different definition of the nature of God could change that view and raise the general consciousness of the world to a higher level in which peace and the happiness of others would be paramount.

In addition, we know far more today than ancient peoples could ever have imagined concerning the powers and intricacies of the visible world as well as the extraordinary subatomic world and the far reaches of space beyond this little planet. Therefore our picture of God should grow to match our increased awareness of these things and reflect our ability to understand more of the Being that controls the enormous complexity around us.

I should point out that symbolic understandings of many ancient scriptures and concepts is not in question here, especially since many were written to have figurative meaning in the first place. But this means that their use as factual guides to the nature of God might now be outliving its former usefulness. Today may be the proper time in the ongoing plan of Creation to introduce new concepts to those who are ready for them.

The Purpose of This Book

Presenting such new concepts is the purpose of this book. It will present to you many aspects of a view of God of which you might not now be aware, although it appears that many great spiritual thinkers of the past received similar enlightened views through direct inspiration. When you reach the end of these pages, you not only will have shared in some of the greatest advances in knowledge of the nature of God than humanity in general has ever been able to see before, but you might have more understanding of your own spiritual relationship to God and to every-thing in the universe than you ever thought possible.

That may seem to be a startling statement, but with recent advances in aware-ness of both this physical world and the world of consciousness, we are in a new era of enlightenment, able to use knowledge that most of our progenitors did not have and could not even imagine. We just saw the problems Galileo had trying to show where this earth fits in the vast reaches of space since the people of his day thought the world to be flat with the universe revolving around it. We also have ways of understanding other levels of existence, other dimensions, and other realms than just the physical, so that a clearer picture of God emerges than was available to any but the most deeply inspired of past peoples.

Now, do not be concerned if you are not in agreement with many, or even most, of the suggestions made in this book. Each of us is on an individual spiri-tual pathway, and all pathways ultimately lead to God. Where we coincide, that is well and good. Where we differ is fine also because the things in this book are just the things my intuition gives me at this point in my development. We will see later how each of us can have different truths and still be one with God. But now seems to me to be the time for presenting some fresh ideas to be pondered.

Let us begin by using the concept of "three" in its ancient symbolic sense of completeness and perfection to look closely at three words generally used to describe God because, when seen in their totality, they form a complete and per-fect view as the number suggests. These words are: Omniscient, Omnipotent, and Omnipresent. They mean, in order: All-Knowing, All-Powerful, and Every-where Present. These words create an awesome concept, but seem not to have been used in their completeness by many religions in formulating their own defi-nitions of Deity. In surveying various doctrinal systems, we find beliefs in Supreme Beings who are subject to ignorance, vengeance, jealousy, anger, contra-diction, whim, weakness, limitation, deafness, favoritism, cruelty, and even inability to accomplish, such as when the God of the Old Testament is pictured as repenting for having created humans, making the resultant decision to destroy everyone and start again with Noah and his family. This makes God seem weak, indecisive, and a failure. Deities are also shown as relating to mankind through fear, punishment, guilt, arbitrariness, and sacrifice of innocents. Surely these fail-ings and lesser qualities cannot belong to the God responsible for creating the bewildering complexity of this vast universe and keeping everything in order from countless galaxies whose outer limits are still unknown down to subatomic particles that can as yet only be imagined. A new and better view is called for if the world is to advance spiritually.

In this chapter, let us examine how the three basic terms can be understood in themselves. Later in the book we will see their use in leading us to a new definition of God that is vital for today as we look at some relevant scientific discoveries, especially in quantum mechanics and the string theory. To finish the book, we will establish for ourselves a practical spirituality that will use these insights as guides to help us develop a higher consciousness in life.

Omniscience

The word "omniscient," or "all-knowing," means that God knows everything. The term not only means that God is aware of every bit of information, but also that God must be the *author* of all information, knowing it first-hand before others state it or can change it with their thinking. Otherwise, there would be something that, for a fraction of a second, God did not know. God is infinite and knowledge is infinite, so God is all the knowledge that exists.

What humans do in their search for knowledge is just uncover things that have always existed in the infinity of God. For example, scientists did not create electricity, but instead discovered something that had been there all along. Even now as we keep developing more and more uses for electricity, we still do not fully understand it. Obviously, it has always been among us in its entirety, just as God has been, but past peoples were only dimly aware of it, and even today few understand it. In the same way, many writers in the past were not fully aware of God's nature, but their works are still influential today. Now, just as we are able to use electricity better as we learn more about it, we will accomplish greater spiritual things as we learn more about the true nature of God.

Omniscience is huge and complex. It includes knowing all facts relating to everything throughout the universe whether in form or not yet in form. It involves complete knowledge concerning the operations of the largest galaxies and of the smallest subatomic realms. It means keeping track of unimaginable quantities of matter in all their changeable states. And it means knowing all thoughts and emotions that have ever existed.

Thoughts are complex just by themselves. They are related to the incredible variety and detail of each life lived on this planet. Everything that we humans have been exposed to, every reaction we have had, every creative idea we have come up with, every relationship we have had, and every word that has ever been said to us are all part of the complexity of our thoughts, even the ones we think we have forgotten from our short-term memories. And everything we now think is instantly affected by such things as our background, past experiences, physical make-up, present surroundings, and the ego-view we and others have of us, which means that every time we repeat what we assume to be the same thought, it is instantly changed by whatever circumstances we are experiencing and becomes a new thought. To be omniscient, God must have all the original thoughts first-hand in their pure state as well as all the various developments and possibilities that unfold. Thus, God's knowledge is not only the facts, but also the changing impressions, opinions, and varying versions of every thought or action that any-one ever has. This is an extraordinarily involved concept, but let me give an earthly example.

Omniscience in Practice

It started with a phone call to my hotel room in Lawton, Oklahoma, as I was tak-ing the summer off from my professorial duties with the University of Texas at El Paso to promote and teach public relations clinics in various towns. A woman's voice said: "Dr. Walker? One moment, please, for Dr. Amstead." "Thank you," I replied, "but may I ask just who is Dr. Amstead?" She answered frostily: "He is the president of the University of Texas of the Permian Basin." "Very good. I will be happy to speak with Dr. Amstead." There were a few seconds of silence, and then a man's voice boomed: "John? This is Billy! I want you to come and be my assistant."

Bam! I was won over. It was obvious that this man had such confidence, strength, and personal power that he didn't need to hide behind formality. Such was my introduction to one of the most extraordinary men I have ever met.

Billy Amstead was established with the University of Texas as a tenured engi-neering professor at the Austin campus when he was asked to build the new cam-pus planned for Odessa and to be its first president. He turned his amazing talents to these tasks with such thoroughness that he seemed to know everything possible about the university plant, its curriculum, and its people. He knew the construction details of every building, the problems encountered in putting each together, the cost of every little thing, the upkeep needs, and the ways each section could be adapted to various uses. He had created many innovations such as moveable walls, flexible laboratories, and academic programs based on self-paced courses. He knew all his faculty and staff thoroughly, including their strengths, their weaknesses, what each could be inspired to do, and just how he needed to inspire each to do it. He was not just acquainted with but knew the pertinent details about all the influential people in politics, business, education, banking, and the like who had any effect on his operation, and therefore knew how to deal effectively with them. What is more, he could usually tell what each person was thinking and what each was likely to do in a particular situation, so he was constantly ahead of everyone else in his planning, foresight, and political savvy. In conversations with him or in meetings, there was no point on which he did not have knowledge and insights superior to those of everyone else, and therefore you always had the impression that you were in the presence of an earthly omniscience.

Omniscience is one reason why God can be referred to as the "One." All knowledge that we humans have, the knowledge we don't yet have, the knowledge that we have forgotten, and results of the knowledge we have had in the past are all contained in God. This means that there can be only one overall Mind, the Mind of God, because all knowledge is in it. If there were two minds, the knowledge would be split between them and one could generate knowledge that the other did not have. All must be One.

Consciousness

This Mind of God is Consciousness, since all awareness is in it. Let me explain this term. When we are conscious, we are aware of our surroundings. We may be keenly aware or we may be a bit foggy, depending on the exact circumstances of the moment. In addition, we may have an awareness of higher vibrations of consciousness or of lower ones, and we may feel them strongly or weakly. As an example, I once heard Joseph Silverstein play a lovely violin solo with the Utah Symphony. As the orchestra faded out in one passage and the notes of the violin climbed higher and higher, filling the hall with shimmering delicacy of sound, I could not help but reflect on the ways many of my students would be reacting to the music if they were there. I felt that some, disliking classical music anyway, would be asleep, meaning unconscious. I surmised that others would have wandering minds, or be only vaguely aware of the sounds. I knew that others who were addicted to heavy rock music had suffered physical hearing loss for some tones and so, even if they were present and fully awake, they would still not be able to hear some pitches and some of the softer volume levels. These concepts of awareness of vibrations in the first place, the ability to sense higher or lower ones in the second place, and the ability to hear them whether soft or loud in the third place are what I will mean in this book when I refer to "consciousness," and the higher spiritual levels of these concepts of awareness I will refer to as "Consciousness." This is for quick identification only since ultimately everything is spiritual, as will be seen later.

So what are the highest levels of Consciousness? Very simple. They are those that relate the most to God. They are what we experience when we feel the presence of God everywhere and when we are fully aware of everyone and everything in shining perfection as manifestations of God. These levels are the highest vibrations felt intuitively as awareness is opened more and more to the nature of God, to the spiritual natures of all things, and to the overwhelming joy experienced in the Presence. Achieving these states is the ultimate aim of this little book.

We all share in this one Mind or Consciousness at various levels through our thoughts and our feelings, which interact with and become a part of It. Otherwise, we might have a thought or an emotion that God does not have and this is an impossibility. All of us share in this Mind because we are all one, and all knowledge and all things are actually spiritual, so nothing can be known or used that is not God. For example, we may think of air as just a physical thing. We all breathe and use the same air. There is none that is just ours alone because what we breathe is a part of the oneness of air all over the earth. This air is continually refreshed for us by the trees of the world in a physical cycle that was set in place by a Mind greater than ours, so air is actually a spiritual manifestation. It is from God and is part of our oneness over all the earth. In like manner our thoughts are all a part of the Whole, and anything we humans think we know, is really knowledge from God. When we become aware of this principle, it becomes a powerful spiritual strength for us to use in increasing the completeness of our own lives and the lives of those around us.

Obviously, such an enlightened view of God and of each other does not allow for the lacks and weaknesses in God and the separations among humankind that we looked at earlier. God is only good, positive, all-knowing, all-inclusive, and peaceful, and all humanity can share in this. In fact, opposite characteristics from those of God do not actually exist since nothing negative can exist. Rather, all characteristics represent points along the continuum of positive virtues, lower or higher though they might be.

On or Not On

Let us look at that idea for a moment. A radio makes a good example of it. A radio is either on or not on, which could relate to our concept of being conscious or not conscious. When it is on, its tuning scale can be in the low or high frequencies, which could relate to our lower or higher levels of consciousness, but the radio is still on. The volume can either be high enough that it dominates or low enough that we have to strain to hear it, but it is still part of the positive scale of sound. If there is a lot of static, the radio continues to be on but only foggily so because of interference with the signal, which could relate to our levels of receptivity of spiritual intuition. All these represent aspects of consciousness.

Now, when the radio is not on, there is no sound, but the point is that there is no negative sound either. You cannot have a minus sound from a radio, just as you do not have a minus side to the characteristics of God. They are all possessed somewhere on the continuum of being on unless they are not on. It is good not to think of a radio as ever being off because that seems to give an opposite to being on. It is just not on. Actually, even when it is in this state, sounds can be induced into its circuitry from the outside because of its receptivity, so it can never be considered as completely off anyway.

In the same way, human characteristics are on sliding scales showing varying degrees of "on" or "not on" just as light is on a sliding scale from no light (from our perspective) to brilliance. There is no such thing as "darkness;" there are only varying degrees of the presence of light. Thus there are no negative personal characteristics but just variations of their "on" natures. There can be ecstatic joy at the good fortune of another or a lukewarm acceptance or even no reaction at all, but there can be no such negative side as jealousy or antagonism. Negatives may seem to exist from our limited viewpoints, but in God, all is at some level on the positive continuum of Good. And what are the highest levels of these characteristics? Just what we saw before: those that are the most like God.

Religious writings that seem to indicate the existence of negative characteristics were probably written by well-meaning and inspired people who used the understanding of the day to make their point for those times. Their limited knowledge or personal agendas led them to make their own applications in discussing spiritual phenomena. In our day, we have greater understandings, greater abilities to comprehend, and more awareness. For example, we know enough of how life comes into being that we can clone animals. Surely our views of living things are distinct from those of ancient peoples.

In the same way, with our view of how emotions and characteristics are on sliding scales of values, we can eliminate the judgments and criticisms that could be involved in our giving life to "negative" emotions that do not really exist, such as guilt, pride, condemnation, or suffering. These are just illusions from our own egos. We can also refuse to give life to the characteristics of being vengeful, jealous, punishing, and arbitrary that have been applied to God in past religious writings. Apparently the concepts of these attributes have been allowed to people on this planet as part of their earthly personalities and spiritual progress so far.

It is similar to our concept of temperatures as being above zero, meaning in the plus range, or below zero, meaning in the minus range. There is no such thing as a minus temperature, of course, since all temperatures are ultimately on one sliding scale and are all in the plus range when the whole scale is seen. It is just our limited viewpoint that makes them seem to be negative. By the same token, there are no negatives opposed to such values as love, forgiveness, and peace, but only higher or lower levels of their positive natures, with the truly lasting values in dealing with God and with each other in the highest realms. When we strive for these positive values, we sense more greatly the omniscience of God.

Omnipotence

Let us now consider the word "omnipotent." It means "all-powerful," so God has all the power. This means *all* the power. There is no power anywhere that the One does not have and, therefore, there is no power of which the One is not the Source. All the power to create everything that is seen by us and everything that is as yet unseen; all the power to keep living things alive, functioning, thinking, and developing; all the power to keep the smallest atomic particles and the largest galaxies in order and to continually create more; all the power to supply functional energy to every aspect of creation; all the power to use the immense forces, the dark matter, the dark energy, and all the immaterial things of the universe of which we as yet have little knowledge is in the Self-Existent One. And, again, since we share knowledge with God because that is where all knowledge is to be found, we also share in the power of the One since that is where all power is to be found. Since God has all the power, any aspect that we may have must be a part of it. This means that there is no duality, with us "down here" and God "up there." We share in the power and the thoughts, and so we are a part of God. And, of course, there is no Satan as a separate being because such a one would have a power or strength opposite to that of God or that God did not have, which is an impossibility. Everything is one with God, and what may seem to be a contrast is still a part of the Totality.

Let me illustrate this with another view of Dr. Billy Amstead. He definitely had the power in the university, and a considerable amount in the surrounding communities as well. Whatever happened at the school was with his approval and usually with his direct knowledge. He had an encyclopedic grasp of everything that was happening on the campus and of how well the people were doing. He was the moving force behind whatever took place, so if you wanted to accomplish anything, you worked with him and shared his power. But what was of great interest to me was the way in which he did the sharing.

In most universities where I have visited or taught, the administrative area of deans and the president is generally considered somewhat off-limits. It is usually set apart and you do not go there unless you have specific business. It is respectfully quiet and a little intimidating. The president is usually tucked away behind various closed doors and is thoroughly protected. But while Billy was president of the University of Texas of the Permian Basin, this was not the case.

The administrative area of UTPB was located across the vestibule from a main classroom wing. When you entered it, the first office on your right was that of the president. His door was usually open, and the desk of his secretary was off to one side so as not to block the door. His own desk was located immediately inside the door and he was so completely visible and accessible that anyone, whether student, faculty member, staff at any level, or visitor, was welcome to walk right in. If you did not go in, he would often wave and call hello as you went by. If you did enter, he would immediately stop what he was doing and visit with you. If you required more than a minute of his time, he would seat you in the chair next to his desk (not in front of it with the desk as a barrier) and would pull his own chair around so that he was almost knee-to-knee with you. It was very clear that this man was instantly part of your thoughts and needs, and that his quick mind, fantastic memory, and depth of knowledge would help you find an immediate solution to your problem. He had all the power and you were allowed to share in it. In that sense, he was omnipotent. And my first impression was correct: he had so much personal power as well as official power that he needed none of the typical external aspects of strength that other people seem to require in a business setting. He could be warm and open to everyone because he had total confidence in himself and in his abilities, and everything was positive.

Power and Freedom

So the power of God is complete and we share in it. However, there is individual development in each of the manifestations of it, such as in people or animals, since this development is within both omniscience and omnipotence and is part of the infinity of creation. We will see how this works later on. Each of us, then, is in a personal stage of development right now as a part of the Totality. It is a little like looking at a picture of, say, President Lincoln that seems to be made up of a vast number of light and dark dots, each of which is actually a complete picture in itself when seen under a magnifier. Part of the nature of God includes being the sum total of all the individual manifestations of the continual creation process.

Entities have the power to make decisions and even to carry them out in what we call free will, more or less. Any thoughts that we have come from our freedom to think, but they still are all part of God since God's omniscience encompasses all thoughts that can ever be. Any power we have comes from God's omnipotence, the source of all power. It is a little like having a discussion about the English language conducted in English. All sorts of comments may be made about grammar, syntax, and vocabulary; experiments in communication can be carried out in different ways; and conclusions about the language can be reached; but it is all still English in its totality. So any power or thought that we use is part of the totality of power and thought that is God. It is not just that there is no power or thought other than that of the One; it is that all power and thought of any sort are *contained in* the One.

It should be pointed out that power is not the same as force. Force, such as military might or fighting, is destructive, uses up energy in moving against things, and causes a counter-force. In the realm of absolute power, nothing actually happens. Power is like the quiet strength of love or the silent atmosphere of gravity: we ourselves may move in relationship to them, but gravity and love themselves do not move. Such power is positive, self-sustaining, and just *there*. In the Judeo/Christian world, the saying is that you cannot break the Ten Commandments; you can only break yourself against them. They, in their power, do not move. In the presence of God, then, there can be no force because all that reigns is the absolute power of the Self-Existent One. The atmosphere is completely peaceful, joyous, and silent. All thoughts are there simultaneously, all knowledge is there, and all happiness is there. Since these exist in full strength, there can be no negativity. In the second half of this book, we will see how we all can attain this peace in our lives as we continue to find God in the quantum.

Omnipresence

The word "omnipresent" means "everywhere present." It can be the biggest obstacle initially to a proper understanding of God because the principle of duality, referring to mankind as being separate from God, is firmly established in most of us. But when grasped, omnipresence can be the biggest open doorway to our fullness of spiritual growth.

The meaning of the term is that God is *everywhere*. This has to refer to all places throughout the universe and within each being or entity in it. There can be no place where God is not. There can be no place to which God only sends a representative or to which God comes in only partial strength because omnipresence means wholly present everywhere. Now we see why people are not in a state of separation from God "down here" trying to find their way back "up there." God, being omnipresent, must be in each person, each tree, each star right now. We have already seen how God is present in every thought that man has and in every aspect of power that he exerts because God is the author of those. Now we see that God is the essence of humankind itself, and is in, through, and as all things because of omnipresence.

Mankind Is Not Evil

This leads to the realization of great positives that can free us from our past fears. We said earlier that negatives cannot exist. We see now that humankind cannot think of itself as evil, because God is in everyone, and God is only Good. Nor can people think of themselves as being alone or of no worth, again because God is in everyone. Nor do humans have to live in terror of judgment, punishment, or separation from God for the eternities just because they do not measure up to some standard that many of them have never even heard of. This is the tribal chieftain type of anxiety, and there can be no such fear where God is. God has not created humankind as imperfect with a resultant plan to punish most people for the eternities because of this imperfection. This would mean that God is an imperfect and wasteful Creator in the first place, and is inadequate to save the entities of the Creation in the second place. It would also mean that God is separate from the entities and enjoys their suffering. Actually, we are all whole, complete, and perfect in our spiritual natures since we are one with God, and we are merely undergoing some learning, growing, and individualizing processes here of varying types for our ultimate benefit. We will all return to the Presence in the end because God's power of Love and Good is all there is and nothing else can exist.

So every man, woman, animal, tree, rock, comet, planet, star, and galaxy is important simply because he or she or it *is*. We cannot criticize or judge anyone because God is in everyone, and therefore our criticisms have nothing at all to do with them but rather with us, showing our own incomplete view of them. It is our own thinking that needs to change and rise to higher levels. The other person or thing is just fine in its spiritual essence, and it is far better for us to identify with and appreciate this omnipresence in everyone and everything around us than to find fault. Just this one idea in itself is a beautiful message, getting rid of the fear and negativism that society and egos feed on and that some leaders wield to keep people in line. People are where they should be on their paths right now because God is always with them and is in charge. If God wanted things to change from what they are, they would change. God is all there is. Your path has now led you to this book and you are allowing me to share in your journey. Wonderful!

There are, then, no evil people because God is with everyone all the time. This is a hard concept to grasp because people want to hate their enemies and to think of themselves as right and righteous. But these so-called "enemies" are just people who are following their own beliefs as everyone else is doing, thinking of themselves as the right and righteous ones, and are on their own individualized paths back to the Presence. Some are ready for the concepts in this book, and some are still involved with other viewpoints. Therefore, these concepts will apply to some people now, but will not apply to others until later. There is no rush. Sooner or later they will apply, and greater ones than these, obviously, and we will all see that there is only Good in the Universe. Since there is no universally accepted definition of evil anyway, there can be nothing for God to punish since there is no one set of rules by which to judge. When we drop this concept of "evil" we come to understand other people better and feel more united with them. Much war could be avoided if people could see this fundamental fact. For now, we should just note that it is only through heightened spirituality that we can see the true natures of others and the meanings of the obstacles that they bring to us in our lives. Note that I did not use the word "problems" because there are no problems; there are only obstacles to overcome as part of our growth.

Consequences

Now, even though God is in us, there are consequences to anything we do or say or even think! If we spend all of our money on books and none on food, there will be a consequence sooner or later, but this is of our own choosing. Consequences are just the outgrowths of our actions and thoughts, not evil in themselves. We have to be careful abut judging things as wrong just because we do not know the whole story. For example, we can hear that a man attacked another, beating him unconscious, and we can say that this was an evil act. But if we find out that the other man was a terrorist trying to take over an airplane in order to crash it into a building with great loss of life, we can say that his being attacked and stopped was a heroic deed. Again, evil is a personal judgment based on ego, and since our limited knowledge does not let us know the value of every act in the big scheme of things, we cannot judge anyone in this way. Just like the radio volume control, everything is somewhere on the sliding scale of Good, and ultimately we will see that everything on earth has to be good because it is all God and God is only Good. When we are fully enlightened, we will see everything around us in its shining Goodness.

Actually, we must make a point here that will apply throughout the book. We may say in one place that God is in us, and in another place that we can arrive at being in the Presence. The difference is a matter of awareness. When we are fully aware of God as being within us as well as within everybody and everything else, then we will see the full beauty of all creation and will understand ourselves as being in the Presence. It is within us all along and our job is to raise our consciousnesses to become fully cognizant of It.

Because of omnipresence, then, it is evident that God is also in the insects, the rocks, the trees, the earth, every star, every galaxy, and all the "empty" areas (which are actually pure energy) among them. God is therefore in the atoms and particles that make up all of them, and so is in the particles that make up our bodies as well as in the thoughts that we have. God is the very basis of who and what we all are. Our thoughts are so complex, based on so many tiny details of our lives, that the only way I could know your thoughts is to actually *be* you. Through omniscience and omnipresence, of course, God does just that, being in, as, and through each of us. All is God. There is nothing else and there is no place where God is not. This is not pantheism since the rocks and trees are not worshipped nor do they contain individual deities, but rather it indicates the omnipresence of God. The extent to which supposedly inert things have a consciousness will be taken up later, but you can guess already as to what the answer will be.

All is One, and everything that seems to be separate is really a manifestation of the One since God can manifest in an infinite number of ways. This is why humans are individual entities, yet are one with each other. The only true happiness comes from seeing ourselves as being one with God and with everything.

So to sum up the three attributes we have discussed, there is one Mind, one Power, and one Presence that unites us all as one. All is God. There is nothing else.

The Three Levels of Physics

Now, let us consider another Big Three that are not so widely recognized. In the world of physics. three systems vie for attention, each able to explain phenomena (and be proven accurate) in its own area, yet none compatible with the others.

Newtonian physics serves us well in our everyday world. According to Newton, only one object can occupy a particular space at a particular time (which we can see in a traffic collision); for every action there is an equal and opposite reaction (which we see when trying to step from a small boat onto a dock, since our stepping forward also pushes the boat backward and we get a bath); a body in motion tends to stay in motion in a straight line (which we can see when whirling an object around our heads on a string and letting go); all bodies attract each other through varying strengths of gravity based on mass (which we can see with the moon and tides); and so forth. We are comfortable with these laws of physics. They reflect our customary view of the world, and give good results in experiments carried out here on earth.

However, Albert Einstein discovered another type of physics that serves better for the immensities of space and galaxies. It is macroscopic, and deals with things moving at great speeds over huge distances. I remember a story about a man who once saw a blueprint of Einstein's and could not figure out what home project he was building with it until he saw the legend written in one corner that said: "One inch = one hundred million light years." Einstein's system of physics is not well known by the general population, however, because it is on a scale that keeps it from being of practical value to the ordinary person on the street. For example, his contention that space is curved and that time is an illusion is on too large a scale to affect everyday life here except in metaphysics.

The thing to note, however, is that these two systems of physics are generally incompatible. What is true in one does not necessarily hold for the other, and experimental research shows different results and phenomena in each. So now we have one system to our scale on earth and a different one to the scale of the heavens. Just a little thought about the symbolism of "three" indicates that there will be a third system at the other end of the scale, namely the subatomic, and, sure enough, there is.

Quantum theory is microscopic rather than macroscopic, and deals with the subatomic world in which neither of the other systems gives correct results. Discovered and analyzed by such well-known names as Niels Bohr, Werner Heisenberg, David Bohm, Erwin Schrodinger, Max Planck and David Bell, quantum theory involves a system of physics that boggles the mind of the person accustomed to the preciseness of the Newtonian world, whose physicists could well have trouble accepting it, thinking it a product of fuzzy thinking. It seems to violate the view that everything can be expressed by exact equations since the equations of quantum theory at the present can only approximate a result. But it has been shown to give correct results in numerous experiments and exists as the third theory of physics in a solid balance with the other two. So we have three rather separated and incompatible systems. It should be noted that quantum physics, as we would now expect, is incompatible with the other two systems. We will see a way to put them together later on.

We will also look at some of the phenomena of the quantum theory and see how they can lead us to an understanding of God, since the subatomic level is the best place to see the basic elements of God's work. In addition, our spiritual view will show that these phenomena are part of the continually creative nature of God and so have always existed. We will also look more closely at what consciousness is and show a little of how it works. We will see that it, like matter, is a part of the quantum reality, so that our *ability* to understand is as much a part of the picture as the *things* we are trying to understand since thought patterns are the realm of God. To grasp these concepts, we need to open our spiritual awareness as well as our rational awareness. The results will be well worth our time and trouble, for a whole new picture of God and of ourselves will open to us, and we will probably never be the same again. Rest assured that the basic theories will be presented briefly and succinctly without much in the way of layman's proof, and certainly not scientific proofs. The reader can find such proofs and longer analyses of these theories in books created for that type of study. In this little book, the reader need just open up and accept these things for the sake of the search for God, without creating mental obstacles or being blocked by preconceived notions. We are entering a new realm here, so let us just relax and enjoy the visit as we start to put these two big groups of three together.

Why Use Physics?

Why should we use physics to do deal with God? I have actually heard an old question debated in classes with much heat and passion: "If a tree falls in the forest with no one around to hear it, does it make a sound?" Opinions and arguments have abounded in such discussions and nothing has ever been resolved. But if physicists had been brought in, their likely first question could have cut right to the heart of the matter: "What is your definition of 'sound?'"

If one person defines sound as being vibrations made in the air, then for him the tree does indeed make a sound. If another's definition of sound is the effect in his brain when the vibrations strike his eardrums, then for him it does not. So our first reason to use physics is that such an approach can help a discussion move toward general understanding and openness to new inspirations, away from personal opinions forced on people as being universally factual, as we saw with Galileo. But the new physics will show such inspirations to be individualized although still parts of the whole, for we will see later how wave forms of possibility collapse differently for each person. It is like one person stating as truth that the stars form certain patterns in the sky. The stars are there, but that "truth" only applies because of one's particular position; someone in a different place, even close by, sees the same stars in different patterns, a different "truth." Yet, each outlook is necessary for, by triangulating three different views of the same stars, we can come up with a three-dimensional wholeness that is more accurate than one view alone would offer. Wholeness through individualities is important, as in the Lincoln portrait.

The story is often told concerning the person who arrives in heaven and is being given a tour. However, when he and his guide pass by a particular walled community, the guide cautions him to remain silent. When they are safely past, the guide explains: "Sorry for that. The folks in there are _____s (naming whatever religious group you wish) and they think they are the only ones here." God, of course, is not partial to one group while shutting out all others. Every individual is important as a contributor to the wholeness. There is only oneness of equals. Generally, beliefs and rules that favor one sect or set of beliefs over another are man-made, no matter how devoutly the members of the sect may believe otherwise. Since one function of organized religion is to limit and control by allowing only one belief system, a second reason for using physics is for us to leave behind, at least for the moment, the tenets of the particular set of limiting beliefs we now profess, opening our minds to a new view. This is not asking people to change their religion because this book is not even about religion. It is about spirituality, and increased spirituality is of value within any faith.

Religion, you see, can be defined as a system of worship having to do with such things as structure, organizational matters, dogmas, rituals, rules, and the like. Groups tend to use varieties of these to separate themselves from other groups. Spirituality means developing an awareness of and a closeness to God and to everyone else, dropping the limitations of specific religious beliefs. So people of any religion are invited to join in this search for higher Consciousness. It is a little like the old saying: "He drew a circle that shut me out, but I drew a circle that took him in."

Now, to take full advantage of this search for the true nature of God, all of us will need to forsake the concept of separateness, at least for the moment, and instead be ready to look for factors that *unite* all things in the universe, which is our third reason for using physics. To do so requires us to venture beyond human partialities, dogmas, and feelings of superiority. Since God is in the physical world anyway due to the principle of omnipresence, an expanded knowledge of physics can lead to a newer, greater view of God as well as to an increased sense of oneness with all there is in the universe without self-imposed limitations. If we tried to achieve all this through religious investigation, it is quite possible that feelings of uniqueness or insistence on adherence to certain dogmas would smother the search.

I remember the story a lady told of herself about when she was badly burned in an accident and spent months in a hospital room on a burn ward with three other people. They were shielded from each other's view by curtains, but they could help and support each other verbally throughout the incredible suffering day and night without relief, especially during the increased pain of the changing of their dressings. They, of course, grew very close as they rallied to help each other through the months of this traumatic period. One day they were visiting and sharing their personal beliefs within the closeness of the group and this woman confessed that she had never liked the people of a particular race. It was part of her because she had been raised with it, and she really felt repelled by those particular people, as compared to the love, acceptance, and oneness she felt from her friends there in the room. There was a pause, and then one man who had been her best friend throughout this suffering, said in a soft voice: "Well, I am of that race."

Thinking in New Dimensions

As we can see, one obstacle to opening a new perspective is that we have often been so exposed to one viewpoint throughout our lives that we just cannot see that there is any other. Here is another illustration of that. I sometimes show students six pencils, and ask them to make four equilateral triangles with them. They get busy and make one triangle using three pencils, another using two more pencils and a common side, and then are perplexed about how to do the last two triangles with only one pencil. I then show them that their thinking is stuck in the two-dimensional mode: I make one triangle with three pencils, and then lay the other pencils across this framework so that three more smaller triangles are formed, each equilateral!

At that point, they usually complain that they thought I meant that all the triangles had to be the same size. I agree that this would be a good thing to do and I urge them to now make all four of the same size. They try, using the same methods, but fail again. I then show them that they are not yet thinking far enough out of the box. I make the one triangle lying flat, then stand up the other three pencils, each with its eraser at one angle of the horizontal triangle and their points together over the middle, thus making three more vertically, all four of the same size!

So sometimes it is good to get our thinking out of our customary realm and into the new dimensions of what is possible. Again, I will do that basing my comments on physics rather than on religion since science is a safe, neutral territory. We need to deal here in specifics that will be understood generally the same way by all, with hopefully a minimum of misunderstanding, which would not be the case if I based them on religion.

This could trouble people who feel that God is above such things and that man can never know enough physics to understand Deity. Others might be concerned that this seems to dehumanize God, an interesting term in itself. But as we have seen, the principle of omnipresence means that God is in, as, and through everything, which therefore includes physics as well as the human powers to learn and discern. When we get a clearer idea of this physical world and the universe in general, we will be guided by intuition to see more clearly both God and ourselves, including who we humans specifically are and how we learn and relate.

The Value of Unity

As we have seen, our view of God right now may be limited by our feelings of religious separation and by our lack of true awareness of what we see or sense, partially because of many things we have been taught so far in life. If we can increase our awareness that all of us are one and are all manifestations of God, made of the same stuff although individualized, we can then increase our insightful ability to gain a greater knowledge of the totality of it all, and thus we will spiral continually upward toward unity in God.

I remember an incident when I was teaching religion in connection with a large university in Los Angeles. All of the different religious persuasions held a student fair on the campus one afternoon during which we manned booths and explained our programs of study with the students in attendance, trying to get them to enroll with us. I noticed that the booth for one major denomination was empty most of the afternoon, which puzzled me because they had a flourishing campus program. When they finally showed up late in the day, I ran right over there to see if anything was wrong. The leader assured me that all was fine and that they had just been occupied all afternoon manning the soup kitchen down-town feeding the homeless. Imagine how we felt, having been discussing our doctrinal differences all afternoon while they were ignoring all of that to go feed the hungry. So let us leave the doctrinal matters aside and see what basic hungers we can address through science.

The key to it all is intuition, that spiritual communication of truth for each of us that we receive directly without recourse to our reasoning power. If we can step, even temporarily, onto a new path of discovery, we can open ourselves to new promptings of intuition that will be our real teachers. Can we know God through physics? No. We cannot prove God's existence. But we can raise our consciousness and rid ourselves of things that block a true knowledge of God, thus creating a field of truth in which intuition, the revealer of spirituality, can operate freely. We will come back to these words later. For now, we will see in the operations of physics (which will be viewed strictly in layman's terms, with no math or equations) a good general picture of God that is far different from that taught by many religions.

But I must caution you that we will also see a probabilistic function in all of this. Without getting ahead of ourselves, we can say that experiments in quantum physics show that matter is described as what it probably is at this particular viewing, not what it is exactly. Now, for large objects, the variable aspect is too small to be measured, and so we ignore it and just see an banana or a truck. But looking at the subatomic level of anything, which is the place of the fundamental power that animates all objects, we will see that we can only estimate that an electron will be found at a particular location or that an entity will have particular characteristics. We can run the same experiment numerous times to get the likelihood of a specific result, but we can't get any closer than that. For this reason, as well as for many others, God must remain a little past man's ability to understand or to know. But we can approach more closely than has previously been possible to a true awareness of and appreciation for the One, and then we can allow intuition and faith to do the final teaching since there is now a clear, open field in which they can operate.

So let us get into our study. It should be pleasant, easy to understand, and able to lead us to wonderful things.

How Light Leads to Enlightenment

Physicists were puzzled for many years by light, which behaved sometimes as if its little photons were particles and sometimes as if they were spread out as waves. Various experiments and theories were created to try to decide which of these forms was the correct one since, in our Newtonian concept of this world, things have to be either one or the other. Then came the quantum theory early in the twentieth century indicating that, at the subatomic level, things can be described as *both* particles *and* waves. In fact, they can be the two simultaneously, but not to the same observer at the same time. Reality depends on the point of view, on how something is observed, which is quite a difficult concept for the Newtonian world to accept. So we will carry in mind that the wave aspect and the particle aspect, although they co-exist, cannot both be seen simultaneously. Right away, then, we see problems with maintaining a strict, limited viewpoint of anything, which can have a symbolic reference to religious outlooks as well.

In fact, we don't deal with specific things at all at the subatomic level. We deal with a huge number of *possibilities*. When we rest our hand on a table, for instance, the Newtonian view is that there is a table and a hand, and they touch other at a specific point, each still keeping its identity. But at the subatomic level, it is unclear where the hand stops and the table begins. There is a fuzziness of possibilities as atoms of both table and hand intermingle. There is a changing variety of combinations of part hand, part table. The closest we can get to a specific view is just a general possibility.

This fluidity in the physical world indicates a need for us to be flexible in our thinking. We remember the parable in the Bible about putting new wine (which will ferment and expand) into old wineskins (which are already stretched to their limit and have lost their former elasticity). Expanding wine can rupture old wineskins, so new, stretchable ones must be used for the new wine. In like manner, we need to put all the new information being made available to us today into minds that can stretch and contain it all as it expands. Maintaining an openness and an enthusiasm to learn will take care of most of this.

As an example to keep in mind throughout the this book, we might remember Plato and the chair. This ancient philosopher and student of Socrates said that when we see a chair here on earth, it is just a physical, imperfect example of the perfect, ideal chair that exists elsewhere. By the same token, the specific manifestations in physics that we will see here have their spiritual counterparts since everything is God, and our minds need to be open and flexible to see these spiritual phenomena when they arise, such as when we talk of gravitons relating to thoughts or of the drag of the Higgs Field in building our energy levels.

Waves and Particles

With all that in mind, let us look again at the wave/particle problem. Trying to follow one specific minnow in its particle form as a school of thousands flashes by takes heavy concentration that loses sight of the behavior and direction of the rest of the fish. But conversely, focusing on the wavy acrobatics of the whole school keeps us from being able to concentrate on any one individual. In the same way, the wave form of a piece of quantum stuff gives only possible ideas of its location, since it can be spread out all over the place, but does give an idea of its momentum, whereas concentration on the particle form of something shows its location but gives only a fuzzy idea of its travel. Since location and velocity are the two ways of specifying something in the quantum world, there can be only possibilities, not fixed facts.

Actually, following a piece of energy is far more difficult than following a minnow because the fish at least keeps its shape even when it moves as part of the wave. In the quantum world, there is a constant shifting back and forth of energy between particle state and wave state, and this takes place throughout the universe. We may think of creativity as being a slow process, but this energy shifting is almost a frenzy of activity as particles are created, disappear into wave forms, emerge again as particles, and continue back and forth so that there is great difficulty even knowing what aspect energy will take at any one instant. The best that physicists can do is deal in the probabilities of having one or the other to work with, which is certainly different from the way things are in the orderly Newtonian world.

Let us set up a camera alongside the freeway. If we keep it still, we capture a clear image of the momentum of the cars streaking by, but since they are just a blur, we don't see clearly the location of any individual vehicle. It just disappears into the wave. If, instead, we pan on a particular car, we comprehend its existence in a particle form, but not its momentum because the background and the other cars are just blurs of varying speeds. If we do not pan successfully, the car is in focus at one instant and then disappears into the wave of cars the next, only to reappear as we pick it up again just as quantum stuff does, and this makes things even more difficult to understand. Again, figuring probabilities is the best that we can do.

As another example, it is like trying to locate a person (particle nature) and also his influence (wave nature) over others at the same time. We can either deal directly with the specific person and know where he is, or we can visit others and see his influence spreading out over them and over other people since he is exist-ing everywhere for them at the same time. As we said, this concept was first applied to light, whose dual wave/particle functions first alerted the scientific community that there was something beyond Newton, but it has now spread to encompass all things, and also has its spiritual counterpart, as we have seen.

Wave/Particle Behaviors

Just one well-known scientific experiment will suffice to show this concept. If a source of photons, which are the smallest aspects of light, is firing them at a screen through a slit in a barrier placed between the source and the screen, the photons act like particles and go straight to the screen and hit in one place. If a second slit is opened, this creates the possibility of particles interfering with each other as they go through both slits, and so now the photons behave like waves, bending as they pass through the two slits and leaving the tell-tale pattern of light and dark interference circles on the screen, the same pattern that fits water waves and all other wave forms. These two phenomena occur even if the photons are fired so slowly through the slits that they do not actually collide or interfere with each other. Possibly they take these positions because of sensing that collisions could occur. Possibly their wave/particle form allows them to behave in both ways, changing from one form to the other even as they travel.

However, we note that if one slit is open, photons will go to a spot to which they would not go with two slits open as shown by its being in a dark part of the wave interference circles. So it is interesting that the photons seem to know ahead of time if there is one slit open or if there are two, and they tend to behave as particles or waves accordingly. They seem almost to have a consciousness of their own, something very difficult to believe in our customary Newtonian world in which only living things have awareness. This can let one suspect that there is a greater oneness among entities than is immediately evident, which shows the need for an expanded spirituality that can account for all forms of life and intelligence.

Now, we may have trouble accepting these concepts at first since they are so different from what we are accustomed to seeing in life, but quantum physics has led to accurate results in countless experiments and so must be accepted as truth in faith by the layperson who does not have access to the scientific or complex mathematical proofs. When we flip on a lamp switch, for example, we rarely stop to consider what the elements are in those inert-looking wires that make the lamp light; we just accept the fact that electricity is "flowing" through the wires and we go right ahead and use it. So in the same way, let us also just accept the idea that something seemingly solid can also have a wave function and an intelligence, and let ourselves be guided into a new world of thinking.

The Role of Observation

Since other experiments have shown that, at the moment of measurement or observation of a piece of quantum stuff, the wave form tends to collapse into a particle form whereas previously it could have been either or both, then we can accept the idea that there is a creative element in the observation itself. The observer or measurer helps create the reality and is not a passive onlooker. This is a spiritual element because the Creator is a part of us, and as we participate in any creative process, we emulate God, but we do it in our own individual way since the wave form collapses differently for each observer. In addition, our "knowingness," or consciousness, is a part of God's omniscience, and therefore the impact of our observation implies spiritual creation and knowledge because God is spiritual and is all knowledge. Thus all things are created spiritually as part of their creation temporally, and we have a role in this. The spiritual and the temporal are one since God is One. This means that anything we think, say, do, or create has a spiritual nature. We cannot compartmentalize, trying to divide things into being either spiritual or secular. All is God because God is in, as, and through everything.

This concept becomes important in addressing the spiritual creativity that is effected through prayers. One group prefers to call them "prayer treatments" because the word "prayer" has come to mean the pleading for what we want to a separate God with a lot of doubt concerning our getting it as so many people do as part of duality. In our new view, we see that we are a part of the One, so that everything is spiritual and eternally present because God is fully and eternally present. Thus we only need to become aware or conscious that the good thing we want already exists for us. The act of opening our *awareness* to that existence becomes a part of its visible manifestation through God the Creator in us. We do not need to plead for it because it is already present. We need to observe it and be aware of it so that it can take form for us.

As an example, we can listen to a symphony orchestra and enjoy the totality of the music, or we can concentrate to pick up the sound of, say, the clarinet, and then follow its musical line. It is there all the time, but we have to observe it to bring it out. So we remember that a thing *already exists*, either in one plane of realization or another, since everything exists in God and, furthermore, everything exists at the same time due to the wave aspect. It is our observation or measurement or imaging of it that allows it to manifest in a particle form that we refer to as "happening."

Of course, by the same token, if we focus on the lack of something, such as concentrating on the fact that we have little money, we help perpetuate that lack through the same creative process, which means that we continue to be poor. Sometimes a lack can be a good thing, such as when losing one job leads to a more fulfilling one when we focus on the positive aspects rather than on the loss. It is only a problem if we get depressed and give up. Our individuality gives us license to choose. The main point is that, as a part of the One, we actually participate in the mind of the Creator as we realize or accomplish anything. If we concentrate on what we lack, then "lack" tends to manifest in our lives. If we ignore it (avoid thinking or speaking of it at all) and concentrate instead on prosperity, then prosperity tends to manifest.

The other day I needed to visit with a good friend who lives down the hill from me. I suggested to myself that he would be outside when I drove up the hill on my way home, even though this was in the middle of the afternoon. He was not, and I was a little puzzled until I realized that I had allowed myself the companion thought that he might *not* be there. So, since I needed to go back down to get something anyway, I declared firmly to myself that he would be there this time, and as I arrived in front of his place he was just driving up. We stopped window-to-window and had our visit. Did God force him to be there because I willed it? No. His coming was already in existence due to the continual creation principle, and I just had to realize that existence for myself for it to actually manifest in my life. It arose out of the totality of God and, as the observer, I gave the wave form of possibility the chance to collapse into that specific particle form.

In like manner, we can manifest a parking place right in front of a store if we are in a hurry and do not have the time to drive around looking for one. I visualize it as already present for me and, almost invariably, it is either there when I arrive or someone is just backing out of a good one. It does not matter to me which person will choose the time to drive away since I just turn it over to God and let the creativity come to my awareness. There is no concept of large or small in such manifestations since all things are present with God, and creativity is creativity. My observation gives the wave form the opportunity to collapse into the manifestation I picture in my awareness, but I do not actually make it collapse, and this concept needs to be explored for a moment.

Things Just Happen.

Things just happen, and simultaneously in every direction! I have heard Dr. David Hawkins say in every presentation of his that I have attended: "Nothing causes anything." He goes on to explain that everything just arises out of the infinity of creation. I did not create my friend's arrival because it already existed. Nor did I make its wave form collapse, but just became aware of it and allowed it to manifest.

Physicists know that an electron can jump to another shell or level of orbit around its atom for no particular reason that we can see. It just happens, and this has puzzled them for a long time. Scientists have now discovered the reason for this behavior, and it is a big one. It has long been postulated that the empty spaces between particles in the atom as well as the empty spaces among planets or galaxies are filled with energy, and now it has been realized that there really is an immense electromagnetic field that exists everywhere throughout the universe. It is constantly pulsating with charges and energy, with creativity and re-absorption, and is the scene of many behaviors in the subatomic levels. Among its names is

Zero Point Field because it is active even at a temperature of absolute zero, at which point all motion was previously thought to cease. In fact, every particle in the universe is in constant motion, exchanging energy, changing form, coming and going. Waves too are active and interactive, constantly setting the scene for reinforcing or dampening each other depending on whether or not they coincide. Creativity and change are constant.

This field, of course, is part of the creative medium of God. It is a vast store of energy forms that arise, interact, and subside again, but since they are all God, they are all one and so are linked even in their diversities. It is not that there is a particle "here" interacting with one "there" because there is no here or there in the oneness of God. That is why particles can seem to influence each other over distances too great for the interaction to travel instantaneously by the speed of light. They do not cause each other to react since nothing causes anything. They both just arise from the continual creativity of God and are linked as one. We humans also are linked to each other in the same ways, but our egos prevent us from seeing what our spiritual natures would see in an instant were we fully aware. Since God is totally present, then all knowledge is totally present and we can develop ourselves to be open and receptive to it. Since all possibilities of creation already exist, our part consists of becoming aware of a particular one in our specific existence here at this time.

Some people speak of God as First Cause, the original cause of everything. This is a very good definition, but perhaps a better one would be to see God as the First Is, or the Only Is. God just is, and everything just is, and what seems to be creativity on our part is just the becoming aware of a specific among many possibilities. We recall from the Old Testament that, when he was on the mountain, Moses learned the name of God as: "I AM." Since Hebrew, like Russian and some other languages, rarely uses the present tense of the verb "to be," the actual use of it puts great emphasis on it. God is therefore the Self-Existent One, the One existing anyway whether recognized or not, the great IS.

Particle and Wave Forms

Let us look at how particles and waves relate to us. Scientists have discovered that when an electron does jump to another shell in an atom, it behaves like a wave first, fuzzying itself out over the various shells as if trying out each by living in it briefly, but *all at the same time!* Then it makes the jump in a particle form. So wave forms contain all the possibilities, and the particle form has the specific. In our particle nature, we are here in this place at this time reading this book and our physical brains are here, but at the same time, the thoughts of our brains in their wave aspects of possibilities are spreading out all over, and our influences, also in wave form, are spreading in ways we know not of through people who may be strangers to us.

Similar to the electron, in our wave form aspect we may review what we have done today and then probe the various things we want to do tomorrow, living out the different paths that we may take to accomplish them, possibly comparing them with what we did today and in times past. We are not creating them out of nothing, but rather are becoming aware of them. When we finally decide on one path, we may go there physically tomorrow in a particle way as the electron does, but we have mentally tried them all today in a wave aspect.

And we tried them all at once since there is no such thing as time in the mind. Time is the lapse between two events when one follows another, but in the mind things can take place in any order and several can exist concurrently. In the example above, our thoughts switched back and forth between what we did today, what we are doing now, similar things that we have done in the past, and what we plan for tomorrow. There is a timeless in this. So as we think of things that have been, that are now, and that we plan for the future, they all mix into a timeless "present." Time, timelessness, particles, waves, all are from the Creativity of God in which we all share.

Therefore, since all is God, thoughts are as real as anything else, and this includes the thoughts about us that are in the heads of the people whom we have influenced or who are ready to receive our influence in the future. (We will look more at the nature of thought a little later on.) Thus, both we and these other people may relate to each other as we sense various virtual possibilities, and then picture ourselves in each reality just as the electron tests various levels, finally allowing one to manifest for us. These are our roles and the roles of others in creation or, as we now know it, becoming aware of what already exists because of the constant overall creativity of God.

This also is an example of the "parallel universe theory," which states that there are infinite worlds on which we exist simultaneously due to the various paths that we and others have taken, and so there are no lost possibilities. We can have them all, just as we saw the electron exist in different orbits simultaneously. It is hard to conceive of such an idea in the Newtonian world of specific physical things, but it is certainly plausible in the quantum world, and we will see more of it later in this book.

Linking

Let us take another step and look at the importance of relationships in quantum theory and in spirituality. Just as chemical elements exist in "families" in the periodic table, and animals as well as plants in phyla, the many subatomic particles also relate to each other in groups, although some of the exact relationships are not yet known. The basic rule of nature, then, is togetherness rather than separation. Now, all happenings in the world of quantum stuff are linked through the Zero Point Field, as we just saw, and are not divided by time or space. Since the Field is all one, events separated by great "distances" (to our eyes) can still happen simultaneously because of the linking.

But those who think that the actions of one particle actually cause the actions of another miss the bigger picture of things. Phenomena, though individualized, actually tend to behave as aspects of one complete whole, rather than as separate entities that influence each other. This should not be surprising because it is obvious that this whole is God, that nothing causes anything, that the Field is a physical representation of the creative energy of God, and that all things are manifestations of the One. Entities are thus individualized, but their basic nature is still that of the whole, and they are linked to each other within the whole. Generally, we humans find our completeness through relationships, since only at the highest levels of consciousness in a total oneness with God and with all that is can we find fulfillment. All is God, all is one, and is interconnected.

Thinking in terms of causes, on the other hand, means thinking in terms of occurrences in linear fashion, one after another, which can knock out the parallel universe theory, can go against the timelessness and total creativity of God, and merely pictures things from our limited perspectives. I once heard of a man who claimed that he could change the shape of the aurora borealis by flapping a bed sheet at it from the ground! Well, he might flap the sheet, and the lights might change, but it is obvious to us that there is no cause-effect relationship. The same applies to everything in the world. Circumstances may favor the occurrence of two situations, but the one does not directly create the other. Everything just arises and God is the sole Source of it. We ourselves are not the creators by forcing the wave form to collapse into a specific particle. We may set the scene, but it just happens. Things are not linear but simultaneous

Creation by Choice

Looking again at the wave function, we remember that an observer does not create reality from nothingness in the quantum world. Instead, he decides on one of the many possible realities that already exist through the wave function and sets the scene to allow it to collapse into that particle reality. Description of a piece of quantum stuff is really a matrix of all its possibilities in a wave form, which collapses into one of these possibilities in the particle form. This is similar to spinning the wheels in a video slot machine game in which we can stop the wheels ourselves. All the symbols are present, but they whirl by in a blur until we stop the wheels and the symbols take particle forms. In life there are several possible "realities" available and the observer selects one. This decision, of course, varies from person to person. For example, one person seeing a boarded up store on the street can feel sadness for the loss of the business that he used to patronize. Another can feel compassion for the people who lost their dream. Another can see the opportunity for a new business to go into the space. The homeless person living on the street can see the chance to sleep indoors that night. All of these possibilities exist at the same time and it depends on the observer to choose which will be the reality for him and allow it to manifest.

Also, we may either see the store itself (particle nature) or its influence in the community (wave nature), such as the effects its products had, or the lives touched by it, by its employees, by its payroll, or by its community service efforts. We either stand in front of the store and see its reality, or we travel around and see its influence, but we don't do both at the same time. As an example, I once read about a photography store that burned down, and the chagrined owner put out a sad sign (particle nature) that said: "Good Night, Sweet Prints." A passer-by liked the spirit of the owner that was conveyed in the sign (wave nature) and supplied funds for him to make a fresh start!

So the quantum world is a participatory world in which we need to deal with both particle natures and wave functions in both spiritual and physical creations to see the totality of all things. This means that a rock is not just a physical creation in a particle nature lying there, but has an essence, a meaning, and a life in its wave form. In the first place, it represents a wave form that collapsed into this particular form here and now, but may be different in another existence. Second, it is actually humming with both wave-like and particle activity because its atoms are in constant motion. Third, it may have an extensive previous history of life in various locations in this solar system. Fourth, God is in it, and so it must have spirituality and importance since God is spiritual. If we see only its present particle nature, we miss its essence. If we regard it only as a physical creation, we miss its spiritual nature. We will see a way to be aware of both particle natures and wave essences later on as we experience further steps in our journey to find God in the quantum.

Other Aspects of Consciousness

Let us return to the concept of consciousness. We saw before that consciousness is awareness, and that it can be either clear or cloudy and focused on either the highs or the lows. Lower levels of consciousness, such as what we call guilt or anger, can relate to destructive behaviors. They do not cause them, but do give an ambience in which they can flourish. Middle levels of consciousness relate to openness, interest in higher things, and willingness to try. This willingness to try is an important value as we will see when looking at the Higgs Field later on. The higher levels of consciousness relate to seeing things through spiritual eyes, with the resultant ambience of love, happiness, empathy, and peace, the things of God. Our whole purpose of life should be toward the development of these higher levels of acceptance and awareness.

Are these higher levels of consciousness limited to living beings? We recall the one-slit, two-slit experiment with photons being shot at a target and how they seem to know ahead of time if one slit is open or two. There seems to be a consciousness level and ability to choose even among inanimate objects. This takes humans off center stage in the intellectual arena and might even damage a few egos when it is realized that intelligence is widespread. God is at the center of the universe, not humans, and where God is, intelligence and higher consciousness are.

Could therefore a rock as well as a light source have some level of awareness? We can remember the idea of parallel universes, and say that the rock seems to be just an inert rock here at this moment, but in another universe at this same instant it could be a living wave form taking part in some sort of creation, maybe never really collapsing at all, suggesting that both the decision-making process of allowing the wave form to collapse and the elements themselves in particle form are from one common source, one energy that is the basis of all reality. Since the spiritual person knows that all is God, this indication is to be fully expected, and since both animate and inanimate objects are part of the One, there are elements of consciousness in them all. None is more important than any other, since all represent some of the infinity of creative power that is God and that is going on continually in this universe and in others. That is why many people are able to identify with nature and other phenomena of this world. And since God cannot be evil, Evil cannot exist. All that can exist, then, is God, and all things that are created are therefore good. It is only our limited, ego-based perspectives that seem to give a different view. The rock is good, the universe is good, all people are good, their choices are good, and all is part of the growth of the consciousness of everything in some way.

To add to this, we may have thought in the past that the brain is the domain of all our intelligence, but we are now finding out that there are brain aspects throughout the body. For example, cells recognize invading germs and, calling upon stored knowledge of past invasions, use the right means to attack them without our thinking about it or even knowing of it. In fact, cells seem to have complete lives in themselves, making many decisions that we might expect the brain to make. Experiments have shown that, even when much of the brain is destroyed, basic intelligence still exists, and is apparently located in the cells. It does seem, then, that consciousness can exist throughout the body, which makes sense to the spiritual person who recognizes that God is omnipresent and therefore is in the cells, in the elements that make up the cells, and even in the nutrients that come into the cells!

There is another use we make of our consciousness. The various parts of our brains do different things. When we look at a car, one part of the brain sees a size; another, a shape; another, a color; another, depth of view; and so forth. What is it that lets these observations become a car to us? There is a consciousness that puts together all these different pieces by taking each sensation and making the decision to fix it in the brain at that moment as the particle aspect of the car, and so the car seems to be a thing, a particle form. But its essence (or wave function) is also there as a part of this consciousness and takes its reality in the view of the car as racy or romantic or as an element of escape from present surroundings. Both views of the car are correct, and are part of its creation for us.

Consciousness is, then, part of the One, and all aspects are different manifestations of it. And since thoughts are the action arm of consciousness, our thoughts help in the shaping of our lives and of our growth. It is up to us to choose the ones that will allow our consciousnesses to open up to their highest levels.

Wave/Particle Forms in Writings

The wave/particle identity gives a clue as to why religious writings are interpreted differently and why there are many distinct religions based on the same books. One person's consciousness may see particle aspects in them, and will thus see facts or real people or true stories. Another person's consciousness may see the wave aspects, and therefore will see many possibilities of meaning, symbolism, resultant effects, and interpretations, without concern for whether or not the people and events depicted really existed in a particle sense. Readers make decisions about what it all means based in great part on their own background, what they have been taught, their experiences in life, and on the emphases that they place on the different aspects of their consciousness, such as the particle form or the wave form. They see what they want to see.

In fact, readers may see only what they have been programmed to see by someone else. I have often witnessed a demonstration such as one in which a noted speaker went into the middle of his audience in order to show them very clearly and up close a picture that he wanted to talk about. Then he went back up front and put an enlarged version on a stand for all to see and discuss. Some of the audience held that it was a picture of a young girl, pointing out specific features to illustrate this, while others maintained that the picture was of an old hag, and could point out the specific features that they saw. The discussion went back and forth and got more and more heated because neither group could see the other group's view. It gradually dawned on them that the front half of the audience saw the girl and the back half saw the hag, and then the truth came out. What the speaker had done when he stood in the middle of the audience was to show back-to-back pictures, a very clear picture of the girl displayed to the front half of the audience and a clear picture of the hag to the back half. What he had put up front was a composite of the two, with essential points suggested but slightly unclear. People saw in the composite what he had shown them in the close-up, and they argued forcefully for their point of view as though there were no other one possible. Since the power of suggestion made them unable to visualize the other picture, they could not realize that both views were correct. How much nicer life would be in the world if we could really see the other person's point of view and realize that we are both just fine.

However, to get back to the writings, it seems in general that the Occidental or Western mind looks for the facts in the scriptures and wants every person and every story to be absolutely true in a physical or particle sense, while the Oriental or Eastern mind (which wrote most of the basic books of scripture such as the Bible in the first place) sees the moral lesson, the meaning, and the symbolism, considering these views to be the actual truth, such as in a parable. One side sees the historical Jesus, for example, and regards Him as having special earthly significance as the Great Exception, while the other sees the Christ Consciousness that anyone can have by dealing in the highest principles, and thus regards Jesus as the Great Example, So there is much to consider in finding spiritual truth in the scriptures, and no one is wrong in what is seen, for each view is a reflection of the path each person is on and the support system each has at the moment.

All in all, it probably could be said that the wave aspect is a truer essence of a thing than the particle aspect because it contains all the possibilities in the matrix including various meanings, rather than the limitations of just one. For example, I have a physical self and people recognize me from it, but it is not the real me. I am not my body or face. I am not my brain, or even the thoughts of that brain. I am the essence behind them all, the one who contemplates and observes the movement of this body through the physical existence and the interactions it has, and I am the one who attaches meanings to it all. I am the continuous wave forms that contain all of my possibilities, and I am the true nature of my spiritual Self, which includes many more dimensions than can be understood in this three-dimensional world, as will be seen later.

My body and brain are never the same anyway from day to day as the thoughts change and the cells are replaced, so it is my essence beyond those things that gives me continuity. But that essence in its highest sensing within the Self recognizes God, sees itself in oneness with God, and finds great joy in the Presence, realizing that in awareness of the Presence is where all happiness, peace, and fulfillment are to be found. So my true Self is spiritual, as is everyone's, and finds great pleasure in sensing God.

Intuition

We can call that highest sensing "Intuition," the reception of information directly from the Source. By our intuition, we can know for ourselves the true natures of things without necessarily understanding them rationally. So all of these details of physics in this book are only to break us free from the restrictions and limitations of our religious viewpoints so that we can be more open to the spiritual intuition that carries the greater knowledge and peace. As we have seen, one of the functions of organized religion is to set boundaries and limits of belief to keep things separated, codified, and organized. We do not need limits spiritually. We are all individuals on different paths, so intuition will be different for each of us, but it will help us achieve the spiritual goals suitable for the different paths we choose. Through intuition we can realize essences, see our relationship to the One as our individual wave natures are realized, and maybe see how our paths might change. Changing our paths, of course, is very difficult to do, given our lifetime of conditioning and indoctrination at the hands of others. But we will see later how a friend of mine named Jerry did it, and we can do it too.

Intuitions, thoughts, feelings, and visualizations are all parts of the same package. Thoughts are not just the chemical processes that occur in the brain. Such processes are physical manifestations to allow sorting, classifying, and remembering, and we can refer to them as the thoughts of the brain to distinguish them from our true Thoughts, the ones that come through our higher Consciousness. These Thoughts are how we sense the inner spiritual natures of things and how we interpret what we see to everyone's highest good. Many people do not really know what spiritual Thoughts are since the ability to recognize them comes from God. Egos tend to block such realization at this point in their development. However, Thoughts are part of the process of comprehension itself because they are how we see the Completeness, which means that ultimately everyone will use them to see and know of God. We will look at how to use them later, but now it is time for one more big step toward finding God in the quantum.

Strings, Dimensions, Gravity, and the Higgs Field

So far in our search, the three different fields of physics have seemed to give lie to the concept of oneness since they appear to be different from and incompatible with each other. As we recall, Newtonian physics is fine for our everyday life; Einstein's physics for the macro-universe; and quantum physics for the micro-universe. Each gives precise results only in its own area, and for God to be One, there must be unity in all the systems of physics. Our solar system is the part of the Milky Way galaxy (described by Einsteinian physics) that contains this earth (described by Newtonian physics) and yet throughout is made up of atoms and subatomic particles (understood through quantum physics). These three systems only seem to be separate because they are seen from our limited human perspective and they must actually exist in a unified state for God to be One. How is this to be?

Fortunately, there is a new theory that gives great promise of being that unifying factor. It may well be the Theory Of Everything (T.O.E.) for which Einstein himself searched fruitlessly the last thirty years of his life and about which Newton knew very little. It seems to form the base of all three systems and is giving great results in early experimentation. Let us see it develop as we look at the concept of space.

Energy and Space

We know that even the biggest galaxies are mostly space. And we know that they are made up of atomic particles that themselves are mostly space. We may have heard that if the actual matter in our whole universe could be concentrated down so that it contained no space at all, it would be about the size of a grain of rice. I used to ask the students in my religion classes: "What makes up most of this table?" Answers would be many and varied, but after a while someone would try: "Space." To their astonishment I would reply: "Excellent thinking." I then would ask them to visualize a hollow ball a hundred yards in diameter, or about the size of a football field, and, of course, a hundred yards high, or about the height of a 30-story building. Then I would suggest that they mentally suspend a small marble in the center of this huge ball. At 15 stories up and in the middle of a ball 300 feet long, the marble would be almost lost from view in all that space. At that point I would explain that if the proton of a hydrogen atom, which forms its entire nucleus, were enlarged so that it became the size of that small marble, its electron would be just the size of a speck of dust racing around the shell of that immense ball! They would easily see that an atom is mostly made up of space. Of course, the constituents of the atom, such as the proton and electron, are themselves mostly space also, so there is really very little matter involved.

But is that space empty? Obviously not, for the atom is a dynamo of energy. An electron is nothing but energy, and for it to remain circling that proton at its immense speed, there must be great energy filling that space to hold it in orbit. There is also the energy needed to hold two or more protons together in larger atoms in spite of another form of energy, their polarities, trying to force them apart (as we see when we try to push two like magnets together). The basic energy of gravity has a role, as well as energy coming in from outside the atom. Science has identified four main forces in physics: electromagnetism, gravity, strong force (that holds nuclei together), and weak force (that breaks the nuclei apart in radioactive decay), and they are all present in the atom. Yes, the atom is mostly energy and yet is mostly space, but since its spaces are filled with energy, we can say that the atom is all energy.

This energy *is* the atom, *is* the body, *is* the star, and *is* the galaxy. It is called "chi" in China, "ki" in Japan, "yoga" in India, and other names in other places, but all know it as the energy that gives life and movement. Proper extrapolation would extend it to inanimate objects as well because their atoms are the same ones as those in living things (a carbon atom is a carbon atom) and are in constant movement even though the object itself seems inert, as we saw earlier in the rock. (Perhaps the martial arts expert who summons chi to his hands in order to break a brick is also relating to the chi in the brick as part of the breaking process.) Since everything is energy, how is it that God is the basis of all that energy? We can find the answer in the string theory.

The String Theory

The superstring theory, generally just referred to as the string theory, is based on something that is much smaller than any particle we have been able to imagine so far, and holds the promise of putting quantum theory, Einstein's physics, and Newton's physics together in balance by showing that all of their elements are basically made of the same stuff.

Modern physics has found that there are many subatomic particles, not just the familiar proton, neutron, and electron. There are quarks (particles that make up the protons and neutrons), neutrinos, gluons, taus, muons, and several more. (Some people include "morons" in the list, but they have their own purposes.) These particles are all arranged into family patterns when measured by mass (we recall our earlier comments concerning the importance of relationships and, no, this is not where the morons are found) and are controlled by a series of weak and strong forces that hold things in a delicate balance. Any changes in the masses of the particles or in the forces that control them, no matter how slight, would create chaos throughout creation. Those who reject the idea of an Intelligence guiding the Universe probably don't have much of a grasp of what really is there.

The string theory suggests that each of these particles is made up of tiny loops that physicists call "strings," possibly one-dimensional or even zero-dimensional elements that vibrate. Their size is estimated to be roughly a Planck length or from 1.6×10^{-33} to 1.6×10^{-35} centimeters, too small to be seen or measured at the moment. They don't break down farther because the real key is not the string itself. The key is in its vibration, including the frequency, the pattern, and maybe even the intensity. Each different entity is made up of strings in a distinct vibrational pattern, and the vibrations are what give the resultant mass since energy and mass are closely related. So, instead of quarks, electrons, neutrinos, muons, taus, rocks, animals, trees, planets, comets, stars, nebulae, and the like being made of different stuff, they are all made of the *same stuff:* of strings, which are *all identical* and vary from one another only by their vibrational patterns and frequencies! It is these patterns and frequencies that give physical objects their individualities and their physical existences.

So, here is the climactic question: what is the power that keeps all of these strings vibrating at the correct frequencies and in the correct patterns, giving identity and existence and mass to everything? Science may not say it, but can you and I say it? Of course we can, and here we go:

It is God.

This answer is to be expected. You may recall a comment made earlier that, in order to be omnipresent, God would have to be the fundamental energy at the core of every particle in the universe. We also said that all existing entities, including humans, are different manifestations of that same energy. Well, it can be seen now that God is the highest energy source and is at the highest vibrational level, keeping each thing, each thought, each atom, each particle, each string vibrating correctly to maintain its identity, and keeps bringing forth new manifestations as a natural function of creativity. This is God, the totally awesome One.

Frequencies and Patterns

How do the vibrations of a one-dimensional string give mass? How do frequency and pattern relate? Well, looking at and listening to a vibrating guitar string, we see that it vibrates at a certain pitch with a certain tone and with a certain power. Its frequency (or pitch) depends on its wavelength (the distance between peaks of its wave); its pattern (or tone) depends on the shape of its wave and of other harmonic waves interacting with it; and its power comes from the amplitude (the height of the crest of the wave above its lowest point). Now, we remember from Einstein's famous equation $E=mc^2$ that energy and mass are related: the greater the mass, the greater the energy. So vibrating energy equates to mass, and this is why there is so little actual matter in the universe (remember the grain of rice?): the universe is mostly made up of vibrating energy. And God, the source of all, is in, through, and as everything, inducing the vibrating energy that creates mass or the forms that we can see and that we call "things."

How can this energy be induced? Here is a simple experiment that anyone can do. Take a guitar, preferably one with nylon strings. Firmly pluck the highest open string, which is the E string. Listen for a second, then dampen it. The sound continues. Do it again, and when the sound again continues, check the lower strings. They will be doing the vibrating, making the sound without being touched by the hands, the vibrations being induced from the higher string. The sound may be in the bottom string, which is also an E string but two octaves lower, or it may be in the 5th string, the A string, vibrating as a harmonic. But either way, these strings will divide themselves so that they do not vibrate at their own pitch but at the higher induced pitch! When strings are in tune, they vibrate with each other and at the correct induced pitch. Note that the other strings, which are not tuned to that note, are almost mute.

Could not God, the highest energy of all, induce the fundamental strings of all matter to vibrate in this way and at the correct pitch? Should the induction in its full strength take place if the strings decide to be tuned to dissonant frequencies? Does this not give us a clue as to how we might attune ourselves with God and thus vibrate at a higher level than where we are now? We will look at these questions more closely in later chapters.

The concept of vibrational patterns gives an answer concerning the source of all the individual characters of people and of things. In music, we note that harmonics and other related sounds can affect a basic tone. For example, the size, shape, and texture of our mouth and throat areas as well as the size and shape of our vocal chords plus the resonating factors of our heads all combine to give each of us a different voice quality or timbre. In a chorus, we may all sing the same note, but each person gives a different quality to it. People can tell who we are over the telephone because of our voice quality or pattern. In like manner, the vibration patterns of our strings all blend together to give us our uniqueness, our individual characters, our many dimensions, which takes us to the next exciting subject.

Our Multiple Dimensions

One of the fascinating aspects of the string theory is that its equations only work in nine dimensions, rather than in just the three dimensions with which we are familiar. When the dimension of time is added, there are ten. Three of these extra six are usually pictured as tightly-curled little spheres at every point along a three-dimensional figure. So to find a particular point on this earth in just six of the dimensions, for example, you have to know its location in the three basic dimensions of latitude, longitude, and altitude (or depth into the ground) plus the three dimensions of the tiny sphere that needs to be pictured as leading off in a completely new direction on that exact spot. No one can quite picture the other three dimensions, although some mathematicians have formulated unusually-shaped figures to give an approximation.

There is good reason why these dimensions are hard to see. String theory now indicates that some strings are open (meaning that their ends are free) and some are closed in a ring shape. The ends of open strings are actually limited by or fastened to the multi-dimensional objects called branes in which they exist, and so they can move around within their brane but go not outside of it. Closed strings are independent, and thus can move around among various dimensions. It turns out that photons, the smallest aspects of light, are open strings, and thus are contained within this three-dimensional world or brane in which we all exist. This means that they not only render our brane invisible to our eyes (since they can travel anywhere in it and thus make no contrast by which we can distinguish it, much like a white-out during a snowstorm), but also that they cannot travel to any other dimensions, and so we cannot see or measure those dimensions. Such dimensions could be located right next to us, but we are unable to detect or quantify them because of the photon situation.

However, we can grasp them in our thoughts, so our thoughts, being things, must be closed strings, able to travel anywhere through any dimensions. Now, only one of the messenger particles from the four basic forces is made of closed strings, and that one is the graviton, the smallest unit of gravity. Since the graviton is an attractor force, facilitating the bringing of things together, it is interesting to reflect on how it might represent thought in the aspect of bringing us together with the things we contemplate. We said earlier that what we dwell on tends to come to pass or, to put it succinctly, what we talk about, comes about, and so is attracted to us. Stay tuned for more on gravitons.

All this means that we ourselves are at least ten-dimensional entities rather than four-dimensional (including time), which means that we are far more complex than can be seen at first. Of course, physicists are talking about spatial dimensions, but since everything has a spiritual aspect, maybe we could illustrate this best by locating a person in more dimensions than just the physical.

Seeing Dimensions in the Personality

The nine dimensions (exclusive of time) give a possibility of three groups containing three dimensions each. Extra dimensions do not need to come in groups of three, of course, but we saw earlier that physicists tend to think of extra dimensions as three-dimensional spheres at the intersections of other three-dimensional figures, so we will use their pattern here. Let us locate the person spatially in each of three three-dimensional groups consisting the physical, the mental, and the emotional, thus achieving a nine-dimensional view. Each of these dimensions can be thought of as a line representing values, so that the physical location of the person, for example, can be somewhere along a combination of the spatial lines of latitude, longitude, and altitude or depth into the earth that we saw earlier. In like way, we can combine this location with the locations along the mental and emotional lines to arrive at a point within the nine-dimensional brane unique to that person at this moment. Obviously, the tenth dimension of time will allow this point to shift continually due to the constant creativity that we looked at earlier, but the concept will be more evident than it might be now. We will look at the eleventh dimension later.

After the physical, the next three dimensions involve the emotional patterns. We can look for emotions that are not the changeable ones of the short-term ego, but rather the basic principles by which life is lived, We can deal in three spatial vectors here also. One could be the serious-playful vector, so that each person is located somewhere along a line between completely dedicated on the one end of it, and completely carefree on the other. If they have neither shading, they are in the middle. Then there is the sensitive-hard vector and finally the outward control-inward control vector. We can say, for our purposes here, that everyone's long-term personality has a value somewhere along each of those three vectors or dimensions, and adding up the three gives us a pinpoint location of that particular personality at that particular stage in their existence.

Then we can look at the mental aspects, and again, for the purpose of our visualization here, we can say that each person is located somewhere along each of three spatial vectors that illustrate different ways in which people think. On the creator-organizer vector, the person on the creator end is involved in thinking of new things using scattered data, coming to conclusions, and making inferences, while at the other end the person just organizes, improves, and deals with whatever is on hand empirically. On the theorist-pragmatist vector, the person on the first end can be a logical, detailed planner, and the one on the other just thinks of whatever solves a particular problem in the shortest way possible. And on the last vector, the individualist thinks only about his own development and success with little trust in other people, being willing to fight them if necessary, while the idealist on the other end likes to reconcile differences and think in terms of social values and of what goals are best for everyone concerned so all can live in happiness.

Adding up the nine points along the physical, mental, and emotional vectors or dimensions plus time, we come up with a point that is unique for each individual at this moment. And just like regular spatial dimensions, we can stand physically next to a person and not see their other six dimensions. However, we can know of the existence of these dimensions through our thoughts, and we remember that the graviton is the only fundamental messenger particle that has closed loops in its strings and thus can travel through other dimensions the way our thoughts can. So the graviton represents how thought can reveal the multidimensional complexity of others. We can also deduce the aspects of these dimensions through observation of the words and actions of others, and so we are not at a loss to understand, but rather can use thought to formulate these dimensions from evidence that otherwise could pass by unused.

You might have noticed that an important dimension is missing from our ten. Let us digress. It turns out that five versions of the string theory eventually developed, causing confusion among physicists for some time. To unite the five, physicist Edward Witten proposed the M-theory which basically assumes an extra dimension or viewpoint giving an overall unity to what seemed to be disparate points of view. This, in effect, gives an eleventh dimension to the string theory. Now, in our model of personalities, we reflect that those dimensions listed are more like guiding principles than ego, but they are still earthly. We therefore may have seen that the one glaring omission in those dimensions is the factor of spirituality. I propose that spirituality be considered the eleventh dimension of people, affecting their overall natures no matter what paths they are on or what traits they seem to exemplify. This effectively recognizes the Self as the true personality. Just as the eleventh dimension in the M-theory smoothes out the differences among the five string theories and shows them to be connected fundamentally, the eleventh dimension of spirituality smoothes out differences due to our various paths and choices, showing us to be connected fundamentally in God. Our ability to see or sense this spiritual dimension is a basic achievement in our search for enlightenment.

Who Are We When We Die?

This brings us to an interesting question that has perplexed mankind throughout the ages: Who are we when we die and what happens to us then?

Some people see themselves right now as only who their egos or their friends or even their enemies say they are. They think of themselves as their body and physical appearance, along with their personality, and they look forward to a literal resurrection in which the body will be perfected and be able to live forever in its present identity. Of course, there is great discussion of what that identity would be. And the opposite side is that such people live in fear that they will miss this one chance to be able to get into heaven and will therefore be condemned to spend the eternities in terrible suffering for not having measured up to something God seems to want.

Others think that the soul goes through repeated reincarnations, gradually improving to the point of reaching perfection and a heavenly existence. The down side is that this life is therefore considered to be full of suffering, with happiness being some far-off dream not available in the present. And there are many other plans and views that we do not need to go into here.

The problem is one of identification with a lesser self. Our body and our personality seem to combine into the real us, and we are loathe to give them up. But we have seen before that the ego-based self with its lower or even destructive emotions, such as anger, guilt, and the like, does not form our real identity. These aspects are just a part of the earthly experience allowed by the probability percentages and uncertainty factors to give us the chance to gain learning and growth. Nor is the physical body our real self. We may have a desire to keep it because some scriptures say that man is created in the image of God, and we think that this means the bodily image. Actually, the God that is in, as, and through everything in the universe and is the source of all energy and creativity has an identity that is far beyond the frail bodies we carry around that are barely able to stand up straight for very long and are subject to a wide variety of ailments, illnesses, and weaknesses.

Instead, we have seen through the eleventh dimension that our real identities are our Selves, the spiritual centers of our beings that recognize and identify with God. When the time comes for us to pass on from this earthly reality, our bodies return to the dust unless preserved with poisons, and the vibrations of our ego-based, separatist selves are also left behind as they are not our real identity. Instead, our spiritual Selves, our true personalities, become aware of their unity with God and with everything else. They do not need to get perfected in order to rise in a resurrection because they are already perfected within us and only await our becoming aware of them. And there is nothing to which to rise because God is in us already and we just need to open ourselves to our complete enlightenment and blend with everything else in the oneness that is God. This blending of our spiritual Selves can again be likened to that portrait of President Lincoln that was made of those tiny dots, each of which was a complete picture in itself, yet giving itself to and gaining its greatest meaning from being a part of the whole. It is in this realization of our oneness with God and with everything else that we realize our complete peace and happiness, whether in this life or in another one.

Which brings us to another aspect. You will recall our earlier discussion of how an electron will suddenly jump from one orbit shell around the nucleus to another level for no reason at all and in doing so, it tries several different levels *at the same time* in a wave form before it chooses one and makes the jump as a particle. The electron seems to live one existence in one orbit, another in another and so forth, but does all of these simultaneously.

Given the huge mathematical possibilities of this infinite universe, we see that there can be parallel universes in which we are all living different lives, making different decisions, and developing different characteristics, such as awareness of spirituality, but doing it all simultaneously. This is neither a concept of one life only nor one of reincarnation, but rather represents a chance to live many possibilities and develop our true Selves more richly.

But it opens a great big question: Who are we really? In which of those existences is our real Self? In which of the parallel universes is our true personality? Is it in this one? In one to come? Or in another one in which we may be living concurrently? Or will we really be a summing up of all the characteristics gained or experienced in all the existences in all the universes added together? Why should we get so concerned about a resurrection from this life when it is only one little piece of the picture?

We might give some thought to the identity with God that we already have and would want to expand as soon as the fantastic happiness that it offers becomes more apparent. Since God is the energy of the vibrating strings at the base of the eleven dimensions of our being, we can as yet in this three-dimensional experience only imagine the depth and power of our total selves as one with God. Possibly we are so much more when the aspects of our other dimensions are added in that our present three-dimensional ego-based personalities will pale in comparison when our awareness are completely opened. Maybe we have so much more to add from other existences yet to come or being lived concurrently that we are nowhere near our ultimate heights. And possibly the desire to be different or independent melts away when we raise our consciousnesses enough to sense our true oneness with God and with each other, relishing the Presence with Its complete power, peace, and happiness. Maybe our greatest fulfillment comes from melting back in the Oneness that is God in our individualized manifestation of it in a higher view of spirituality and joy.

Thoughts as Related to Gravity

Now, in this present life, it is only through our thoughts that we can begin to penetrate these other dimensions and possibilities to get a glimpse of who we really are, which brings us to thoughts and gravity. Probably most of us share Newton's idea that gravity is an attraction between two bodies. Einstein showed it to be the same force as acceleration. Some experiments in the quantum have indicated that gravity may result from a pushing effect where gravitons, messengers of gravity so small and weak that they have not been seen yet, move between two bodies in waves taking up space and allow the larger activities of the Zero Point Field outside them to drive them together. Whether or not this is so, we remember that the graviton is the only messenger of the four major forces that is made of closed strings, and thus can travel throughout the dimensions predicted by the string theory. Possibly, since the nature of the graviton is to attract, and also since everything has a spiritual counterpart, they could represent thoughts and the things to which we are attracted. We use light with its little messenger photons to represent enlightenment, the realization of truth and God, and so we could also use gravitons to represent the attraction between the object of thought and the thinker.

We remember that the thoughts running through our physical brains are electro-chemical reactions involved in sorting, classifying, and extracting meaning. Our true Thoughts are beyond the brain. My body and brain will die but I will continue on, and so my Thoughts must be of some other stuff than tissue and chemicals. Is there a spiritual side to thoughts?

Well, we note that the main attraction we have is to God. All people have a desire built into them to worship something, and the only differences among them are the paths they take to do this. Actually, all thoughts are of God as we see in God's Omniscience. We are attracted to God through our thoughts which can also go beyond our apparent three-dimensional reality. Since the ethereal world seems to exist side by side with the three-dimensional world, and since God is all there is throughout the universe, it is obvious that there are spiritual aspects to what seem to be earthly phenomena. The string theory started out as a way of relating with the strong force in nature, the one that holds the atoms together, but physicists soon found out that it is really related to gravity, that elusive quality that has defied description or capture for all these years. Gravitons are at the base of the string theory just as thoughts are at the base of our relationship to God. And the graviton, having zero mass, is the string exhibiting the calmest, gentlest vibrational patterns. It is a blank canvas on which one can create through the mind, since everything starts with a thought and builds from there. Actually, gravity only seems to be weak in this world. Possibly its energy is partially in the other dimensions to where other messenger particles from here cannot go, and so it may be very strong when all of our dimensions and aspects are put together. It is hard for people to grow within this three-dimensional framework, and so we need to let our thoughts related to God help us grow in the other dimensions to where the graviton can indeed go.

The Higgs Field

This concept of growth takes us to the Higgs Field, the last point in our journey through the quantum in these pages and the aspect that gives us the spiritual reason for our being on this earth. To understand it, we have to remember that everything is energy. The concept of mass is a convenient way to refer to a quantity of energy because through it, particles clump together into concrete forms that we can detect with our five senses and which are easier to understand than the concept of pure energy. We know from the string theory that there is not mass plus energy because all is energy at its most fundamental level, that of the vibrations of its strings.

We have already seen how the electromagnetic field with its photons extends throughout space, and it is very familiar to us in these days of radios, televisions, and cell phones. The gravitational field with its gravitons also extends throughout space, but it is less familiar because we still have trouble grasping how it works. And, as we would expect, there are other fields along with them. One of them is the Higgs Field, named after Peter Higgs, a Scottish physicist. It apparently was formed along with the universe, but cooled off in the frigidity of space in an unusual way: it condensed into a non-zero value field throughout space. It seems to have zero energy but not a zero value. According to models, its boson (a particle with a particular spin) will interact with another particle because of its non-zero value and will create a force between them, with the result that the particle gains mass from the interaction, similar to how a muscle is built by working against a resistance. There are differences as to whether this only happens with simple, elementary particles or with more complex ones, but for our spiritual search the result is the same. Imparting mass to particles equates to adding energy to them since mass is energy, and this mass represents the energy of the vibrating strings. The particles keep their energy because the Higgs Field exists everywhere and so the particles cannot get away from it. In fact, if it were not for the field, no particle would have any mass.

Now, the trick is that this only occurs when the particles are accelerating, not when they are floating freely. As the particles increase their speed, they are subject to what we can call the "drag" of the Higgs Field and they gain this mass or energy. Going back to building muscle, we don't gain much by sitting around, but when we make a point of exerting ourselves and pushing our limit, we gain the strength.

Since everything has a spiritual component, we can see an important aspect here. We have our own Higgs Field that imparts higher energy to us, but only if we are accelerating. If we are just floating along in life, we do not gain spiritual strength or higher vibrations. If we are accelerating, trying to increase our spirituality, we keep adding energy and then more energy to that energy, and we rise in our levels of consciousness. The higher the energy we get, the greater the drag, and so the greater energy we can get by overcoming it. This is possibly why the increases in vibrations from the lowest destructive ones to the highest attainable ones of pure love and oneness with God as described in Power Vs. Force by David Hawkins are in exponential form, wherein the curve rises more steeply the farther we are along it. Much more is gained by each step in the higher frequencies of vibrations, possibly due to overcoming greater drag due to the energies already accumulated.

Actually, this is why we are here on earth in the first place, which answers that age-old question. We are here to take advantage of the opportunities God has set up through the totality of creation to grow in consciousness and spirituality and to gain the experience that comes from overcoming obstacles, all as part of the constantly creative nature of God. Spiritual growth is not just supplied to us. The old phrase comes to mind: "God helps those who help themselves." I remember the story of the young salesman trying to sell a set of encyclopedias on farming to an old farmer, going on and on about how much better he would farm with the knowledge in those books. "Well, son," said the farmer, "I really don't need those books because I'm not farming half as well as I know how to right now!" Farming means growing things, so how are we doing? Are we growing our spirituality half as well as we know how to right now? To grow with the energy of the Higgs Field takes effort and acceleration, and in the last part of this book we will look at ways in which we can do exactly that.

But first, let us look at some ramifications of all this: What do these discoveries do to our former concept of a personal God? What is the role of emotion? How is God not just a machine? How can we actually achieve a higher union with the One and with each other through this knowledge? Are there specific steps that we can take? Let us find out.

What About Character?

Let us address some concerns that might come up with this new view of God since it seems to be so much at variance with prevailing ones.

Man tries to personify things. He refers to his inanimate objects as "he" or "she," sees pictures of people and animals in the clouds, and even arranges the stars into shapes of living things and then invents humanistic stories about them. Throughout history, he has also personified his gods, creating them in his image as we have seen, giving them characteristics that he himself feels, such as jealousy, anger, inconsistency, and the like. Some people even say that the only reason this earth was created was for God to bring forth the crowning glory of the Creation, Man, and that the universe revolves around him.

Well, this view may be a little presumptuous. Let us take just one example. If the age of the earth to this point in its history were equated to a 24-hour clock, we would see that man doesn't come onto the scene until thirty seconds before midnight. Unfortunately for his ego, the earth as made by God existed very well without him all the other 23 hours and 59+ minutes. Isn't there more to God than just having created man on this little planet? Does God really have to look like a man even though most of the vastness of creation has no relationship to the figure of a man? Is it our vanity that insists that God and we must look alike? What does "alike" mean anyway?

What is a Person?

Earlier we saw a basic truth: each of us is an individual manifestation of the Wholeness that is God and each is pursuing his or her own path. If a person decides to stop floating along with old, familiar religious practices and instead accelerates and starts out on a different path toward enlightenment, the spiritual Higgs Field takes over, energy is added, and old religious practices generally either fall away or take on a glowing new meaning. The person can feel released from earthly restrictions to achieve the spiritual fulfillment that being an individualized manifestation of the One makes available when the person becomes aware of it. This is not easy. Old habits, customs, ties, and emotions don't change easily overnight, especially if we insist on hanging on to them with just a few alterations.

We have seen that a "person" is not just the flesh-and-blood object that we think we perceive before us. That form is the particle nature that takes this shape right now as perceived by our limited vision that cannot see other dimensions or comprehend the compounded effect of other existences. We have seen that the wave function contains more of a person's totality, and since the wave function allows multiple aspects of the person to exist simultaneously, we may be looking at only one variation of the true person when we see the particle form.

We could say that the real person is an essence or wave form that we just refer to with a name and an appearance, as we have indicated earlier. Or that a person is the totality of his or her dimensions and existences. Or that the person is the influence or effect made on others. Or that the real person is a manifestation of God, a part of the One since the One is in him or her. Or, possibly, that the person has his or her real existence and meaning as a part of the Energy that is God, existing continually as a portion of that Energy whether in front of us in a particle nature or not. Or, of course, we could say that all of these are true at the same time. Possibly the best way to understand ourselves, others, and God is to see this all-encompassing oneness and to make ourselves a part of the totality of the universe. This is how mankind can be in the image of God, for God is the totality of the universe.

The vibrations of God's energy are vital to this view. Higher vibrations from greater energy in the physical realm relate to positive attitudes, good health, and greater spiritual awareness. Lower vibrations relate to poor health, depression, lesser feelings, and lower spirituality. When vibrations get low enough, death can occur because the system just stops operating. For example, every thought we have is accompanied by many neurotransmitters in the physical body. Endorphins, chemicals that make us feel good, go with positive, uplifting, loving thoughts, including our deep thoughts in meditation. Stress chemicals go with angry, fearful, or depressed thoughts, affecting the functions of the body and lowering our vitality. So raising ourselves closer to the positive oneness means to raise our vibrations and thoughts to put ourselves in tune with the highest values, the values of a dynamic life full of light and warmth. One of the best ways to elevate ourselves is through intuition and awareness of the reality of the vibrations.

Emotions

Here is food for thought: every large culture in the world of which I have knowledge has music. There seems to be a universal need to relate to the vibrations of music, which can bring out the deepest emotions in us. Could this not possibly come from the fact that we are made of vibrations, the vibrations of the strings? When we identify with these vibrations, we identify with God, the Source of them all.

But we equate music with emotions, so is there room for emotions in our new view of God? With great music, some of us feel that we are touching something beyond, something sublime, which is a word referring to the awakening of uplifting emotions from awe-inspiring beauty or grandeur. Longinus, of the first century, spoke of the sublime as being related to a greatness of spirit that is sensed in an author himself, not just in his subject, and he points out that greatness, including greatness of size, gives rise to intense feelings.

As a modern example of this, a string quartet playing the second movement of a certain work by Samuel Barber can gives rise to some feelings of the sublime because the listener senses the greatness of the music and moves with the vibrations. But a full string orchestra playing the same movement, usually called the "Adagio for Strings," can allow much greater emotions because the larger size of the orchestra creates an even greater fullness, richness, and volume of sound.

Now, since God is the greatest of all, and has the most "greatness of spirit," it is clear that the highest sublimity exists as we realize our close relationship to the One. And since God is in us and we are but manifestations of the One, then these intense emotions themselves are a part of God. So God definitely has emotions, and greater ones than mortals can have.

Actually, since our emotions can be considered the mental activity arms of our feelings, the higher the vibrations of the feelings, the more aware we are of God in our mental activities, our thoughts. The lower the vibrations of the feelings, the less awareness we have of the great vibrations of God. God can only be comprehended through positive feelings, intuitions, and high-vibration mental activity, and setting these by growing through the Higgs Field is our responsibility within the free will of our individual manifestations. It is a great part of why we are here in this earthly existence.

A great key to all this is intuition, that sense of awareness and knowing that comes directly from the God essence within us through our feelings, and thus is outside of rational thought. Since we cannot know the exact nature of anything at the subatomic level due to the probability factors and the uncertainty principle, we rely on a sense of knowing based on creative receptivity, which is the ability to receive thoughts directly from our inner spiritual natures attuned to God, and to make choices based upon them. It is a sense of the Divine that we can feel in ourselves and can also realize in animals, plants, and other creations. It is only through the intuition that we can truly know of God and, as we said earlier, the purpose of this little book is not to prove the existence of God, but to use examples from physics to create a field of truth in which the intuition can function freely to help us realize God for ourselves without human-imposed blockages or limits.

So God, in spite of possibly not having the face of a man, is not a machine, but is the highest and best in creativity, love, and sensitivity. We humans have but small manifestations of these, with far less ability to feel and express. For example, we think we feel love for others, but often find ourselves criticizing our loved ones or being selfish with them. God represents the true and enduring aspects of love. which include constant care and desire to give. We will look at ways to achieve these abilities ourselves later on.

A good way to help realize oneness is to set our Consciousness to the higher vibrations that come from feelings of love, compassion, acceptance, sensitivity, and spirituality, continually recognizing and vibrating to the God in us and in every other being or object. It is difficult not to like others when we see God in them, even though we may disagree with what they are saying or doing at the moment.

In addition, we can identify with plants and animals by recognizing that God is in them also and that they have emotions, an interesting subject in itself. We can appreciate and properly care for the earth itself, for God is in it. We can hug a tree, make an pet happy, appreciate beautiful growing things, recognize the values of other people, and be grateful for all of the wonderful things around us and

for the spirituality that allows us to sense their beauty. When we have full awareness of the Presence, everything will be beautiful to us and our enlightenment
will be complete.

To help achieve these higher levels, we use meditation to open our awareness
to the nature of God and to who we really are so that we can receive insights
through our intuition. These insights will be different for different individuals,
depending on where each is on the path, so we need to do this step in the freedom of being alone. The more we listen to these intuitions, the more sensitive we
become and therefore the more able to receive additional intuitions. We will
devote a whole chapter to meditation later on.

Is Interference a Good Thing?

Since we are all individualized manifestations of God, we may feel that everyone
has the freedom to develop in any of an infinite number of ways, so long as there
is neither hurt nor harm to anyone else since that would interrupt that person's
development. I have often heard this phrase: "Your right to swing your fist ends
where my nose begins." In a personal way, we may feel that we want to develop
our characters and spirituality without being interfered with by other people. But
it is hard to know whether or not such interference is actually part of our learning
process here on earth. I heard a minister tell of a Buddhist monk who was impris-
oned by a foreign government and badly treated for several years. When he
emerged, he was asked what his worst moments had been. He replied that once
or twice he almost lost compassion for his captors! He put a positive growth
aspect on what some would call an evil situation. Now, should he have been
allowed to develop his peaceful enlightenment free from this imprisonment and
torment, or were these necessary parts of the growth toward enlightenment that
forms his main reason for being in this particular existence?

Since we do not know the answer to such a question, we need to look at his
response for a clue. He may have been in prison physically, but his mind and
spirituality were free. He used the time to develop internal strength and resolu-
tion much like we saw how a muscle is developed by working it against a resistance. A resistance cannot necessarily be considered evil because it leads to a
stronger muscle. Therefore we cannot condemn an outside or physical environ-
ment as bad because it may well have a role to play in our spiritual development.
An illness might give us a chance to back off from our busy ego-centered life to

contemplate spiritual matters. A job loss may open the way to a new career. At one point in my life I suffered five major traumas within one week, any one of which is considered seriously life-changing. I just picked myself up and started off full-tilt in a new direction, and I have been much the better for the experience. We have to remember where all the power resides (omnipotence) and that God is in and as everything (omnipresence), including ourselves, so everything is in order. Some people say that everyone is entitled to have a perfect body and perfect health, but we do not know the proper definition of "perfect" for that person at this point in his or her development. All we know is that whatever occurs is part of a great and wonderful plan of Creation (omniscience) and we look for the ultimate Good in it.

This act of looking for the good and the positive in a situation so that we can grow rather than for the bad so that we can criticize, condemn, or feel discouraged is a key concept. We need to remember that no one can change our vibrations by making us angry or sad or even happy. The truth is that we *choose* to have such feelings regardless of our outside circumstances or the actions of other people. The brilliant Russian engineer Jakow Trachtenberg escaped much of the horror of the Nazi death camp he was in during World War II by retreating into his mind, where he worked with mathematics. Having very little paper, he invented a speed system of arithmetical calculations that could be done in the head. Today, his mental system enables anyone to be a calculating expert without a computer and is a great help to children who are having problems with arithmetic in school. He decided to be productive in the face of hopelessness, and maybe his imprisonment was a necessary part of it. There are no accidents. Outside interferences are obstacles to be overcome to attain growth, not problems to discourage us, and certainly not errors. Much of our spiritual increase depends on understanding that.

However, I would suggest that beings of peace, spirituality, and enlightenment should place no obstacles to anyone else's personal spiritual development. This means that I should not force my beliefs or rules on you any more than you should force yours on me. I recall the words of Benito Juarez, the Zapotec Indian who twice was president of Mexico: "Respect for the rights of your neighbor is peace." The world would be a vastly different place if just this one characteristic reigned. If everyone recognized that each person is an individual manifestation of God and is on an individual and important pathway to oneness within diversity, slow though it may seem to be, then we would all appreciate and help each other find peace and fulfillment.

You might want to keep in mind the chorus of a song that I wrote:

> God is Love and Peace in our lives,
> We feel the Presence day by day,
> We hear the Oneness call.
>
> God will never cease in our lives.
> Deep in the silence of our mind,
> Leaving the noisy world behind,
> There in our higher selves we find
> God is Love and Peace,
> And that's all.

PART II
The Practice

Spirituality of Oneness

In the first half of this book, we looked at God generally through the intellect. We saw data that our minds analyzed, sorted, processed, and filed in various ways. Our minds may have even drawn conclusions from the data in relation to our individual frames of reference. This is what the mind does in a step-by-step form of logic and reasoning. So it may be that we have achieved a new, logical concept of God, but there remains much more to be done in order for us to really *know* God.

The intellect can understand a great deal *about* something but cannot really *know* the thing because to do so it would have to *be* it, as we said earlier. We may think we know our spouse or children or co-workers, but in reality we only see a part of them, and even that through the limits of our own limited perspective, and even beyond that through what they are willing to show us or what we are willing to see. We might draw conclusions about them and about what we think they will do under given circumstances, but these conclusions can be quite a bit off the mark because we only see what *we think* they are. Again, to really know them, we would have to *be* them. We know how difficult it is to even know ourselves even though we *are* ourselves because we have so many areas of denials, false impressions, and lacks of awareness occasioned by the ego's desire to make us seem great and separate that we are blocked from the true knowledge of ourselves. How much less, then, can we know about others for the same reasons? Yet we go on making judgments about them from our limited perspectives, being unhappy with them, and spiraling downward to lesser vibrations through our lack of awareness of their true natures.

Who Are We?

To sum up what we saw earlier, if we really knew ourselves and everyone else around us, we would see all of us as spiritual beings on various temporary human pathways to enlightenment as part of the infinity of creation that is God. We would see all of us as good, all of us as one, and we would rejoice together in the

63

peace and love that God is and that we all are in our true Selves. In the beginning of this book, we needed the intellectual approach to help us see that there are other levels of consciousness and to get a glimpse of the stupendous Entity that is the Basis of all. Now, in the second half of this book, we will look at ways in which we can actually *be* this spiritual fulfillment, becoming aware of our true Selves through doing, and finding beauty in it all.

Take one hand off this book and point to yourself. Just physically point to yourself. If you are like most people that I have done this with over the years, you are pointing at your heart region, not to your head. We know that we think with our brains, but we say that the seat of our real self is the heart, the area of emotions, feelings, love, and appreciation of beauty. As we said, emotions are feelings put into thought and are characteristics of our visible selves. Enlightenment comes not just from our assimilating and understanding things, which is part of the intellect, but also from our doing, feeling, and trusting, which are things of the heart.

However, since emotions themselves are fleeting and variable, and are often based on our egoistic, earthly selves, it is better to let our "feelings in thought" come from our highest Thoughts, the seat of higher feelings, and be set up as principles, principles that we can adjust to guide us steadily and continually while still being sensed as feelings.

Let me explain the difference. In ancient city-states of what is now Greece, a pure democracy (of sorts) was practiced in which those eligible to vote gathered in one place to signify yes or no to a proposal. But emotions could permit the vote to go one way on one day, and the opposite way on the next, so there was no stability. The founding fathers of the United States wanted a democracy but wanted stability also, so they created the Constitution as a steadying factor. Democracy is practiced in America, but rather than being based on emotions that can change quickly, it is based on the firm principles of a Constitution that is hard to change. In the same way, we would do better creating quiet, steady principles for our guidance rather than changeable emotions.

For the sake of simplicity in dealing with such principles, let us look at two terms that we are using to describe ourselves and our relationship to God: "self" and "Self." We could get into such terms as the id, the ego, and the super-ego, among others, and, indeed, we need to refer to the ego often to clarify aspects of personality, but self and Self are easier to use because they are not colored very much with previous definitions that affect our understanding of them.

The Ego and the Self

So I will use "self" and "Self," and we can start right out with my definitions. By the "self" I refer to our physical and mental being, including the physiognomy and personal attributes that other people think we have and by which they identify us. The physical body is our instant identification to others. Our face, height, build, and voice make each of us a distinct being to the eye and to the ear, different from anyone else. Our ego is a list of personal characteristics that serve to identify us in our behaviors and relationships. We remember, however, that they also serve to limit us to fixed ways of thinking rand doing, inhibiting us from growing spiritually. Of course, the ego treasures such identification and separateness since, without them, the ego feels that it ceases to exist.

So then, the ego is the idea that we carry with us of who we are. It is a series of definitions, some of which are supplied to us by parents, some by siblings, some by friends or teachers or enemies or strangers or even by ourselves as we observe our own reactions to various situations. A little thought shows us that such definitions by so many different people are generally off the mark, since people usually understand and judge only from their own limited perspectives and therefore do not really comprehend anyone else. Unfortunately, we don't comprehend ourselves very well either, especially when we are very young, and so we accept these judgments of others as true and we let them define us. As a result, we spend our lives floundering around in erroneous definitions, feeling frustrated and unfulfilled.

It is only when we rise above the limitations of these definitions that we discover the spiritual entities that we really are, a situation that the ego fights against constantly to be able to keep its job. It sees our unification with God as a loss of identity. In its earthly view, it just cannot realize the importance of spiritual oneness and so tries to block the emergence of our true Selves as one with God. Yet when we see white light, we are witnessing the effect of combining all the different colors of light into one. The individual colors are still there, as can be shown by dividing them out through a prism, but when they are combined into one, they make a brilliant whiteness. In like manner, we can content ourselves with being individuals just as various colors are individuals and certainly are beautiful, but the brightest light, the most brilliant, the one that illuminates (enlightens?) the best, is the shining whiteness of a unity of all the colors. So ego death is the greatest thing that can happen to us because its ideas of separateness, uniqueness, and our being better than our peers can keep us from feeling this shining oneness with each other and with God. If we are in competition to prove our worth and to survive as separate entities, we cannot feel close to others or see their spirituality. We feel that we must carry the idea that we are right and they are wrong, as opposed to our both being entities of oneness and therefore both being on track.

In addition, along with the idea of the self as being separate come some identifying words that often mark this need for difference and uniqueness, although they too are just illusions: greed, envy, jealousy, covetousness, anger, pride, judgment, criticism, righteousness, obsession, pomposity, belligerence, guilt, suffering, ambition, forcefulness, and just plain old selfishness, which attribute has been singled out by more than one writer as the greatest cause of humankind's unhappiness and feelings of separation from God. The self with its feelings of dualism is really the biggest obstacle to our spiritual progress, but we can also be grateful for it and for this human experience with it, for we need time with our human selves in order to become aware of our real fulfillment. We just need to keep the ultimate goal in sight and remember that our Self is our true identity, and the bright light of oneness is our goal.

The Self and Spirituality

What, then, would be the definition of the "Self?" Quite at the other end of the scale, of course. If the self is our expression of separation and uniqueness in the material world, then the Self is the spiritual side, the part of us that feels oneness rather than division; love and goodwill rather than selfishness; sharing rather than greed; happiness in the success of others rather than envy; and peacefulness and calmness rather than the agitations of the ego struggling to maintain its dominance. The Self is the part of us in communion with God and, indeed, actually feels itself to be in the Presence whenever we set our intention to that purpose, such as in meditation or in living a benevolent existence. The self deals in force to get what it wants, such as pushing, coercing, compelling, and the like. The Self deals in power, the still, silent power of the Presence that gives energy rather than takes it away; that is calm, confident, and unmovable; that just exists and is All in All. The Self is aware that the only real peace is the spiritual peace of the Presence, which is the domain of the Self in its oneness with God.

Let us take just one example of the combination of individuality with unity: the religious practice of passing the sacrament, which is the central point in many churches. Over the years, I attended meetings of probably fifty different congregations of one particular faith that insists on unity in everything that happens in its meetings, and yet I never saw the sacrament passed to the congregants in the exact same way in any two of them. People carried the elements differently, moved differently, offered them differently, stood differently, said things differently, and did things in different order. This is not to say that any of them were wrong. They did not seek separateness as the teenager might with individualistic clothes and music. They were actually all one in purpose, and their individuality in carrying out the oneness was a natural variation. The oneness was still there.

So now we can see why this book carries the subtitle: "Spirituality of Oneness." The phrase actually carries three definitions based on different interpretations of the word "one:"

1. it refers to you as one person in your own spiritual work;

2. it combines everyone and everything into one;

3. it is God, the One.

Any spiritual practice that combines these three concepts brings a person closer to enlightenment and to the peace and presence of God. In the example of the sacrament, those participating were individuals banding together in oneness for the church service as they all focused on the One, which was God.

Let us see some ways in which our Self can be paramount in our lives by calling upon EMILY to help us.

EMILY

In setting out to establish the next portion of our pathway toward spiritual fulfill-ment, we need a guide. This guide needs to stay with us all the time, show us the way constantly toward our chosen goals, and yet be flexible in our changes of direction or specific means. My guide is EMILY.

EMILY is my constant companion, inspiration, and source of guidance. EMILY has given me greater happiness, comfort, and peace than any other guide I have had in my life. I am happy to share EMILY's expertise with you, either so you can use all the great benefits offered, or so you can be inspired to find your own companion according to your individualized path. EMILY is very adaptable to different life styles and philosophies, however, and it might be well to check out thoroughly the possibilities my guide has to offer before jumping to another.

EMILY, of course, is an acronym, a complete package, representing:

> Enlightenment—the goal
> Meditation—the medium of preparation
> Intention—the way we treat ourselves
> LOVE—the way we treat ourselves and others
> Yielding—the way we treat ourselves, others, and God.

Each of these elements will be considered at length in the following chapters as you begin to establish your own path to spiritual fulfillment and peace.

EMILY Is For Everyone

As to why EMILY has to be different things to different people, we need to recall from our discussion of quantum physics the role of the observer in effecting something. A wave form collapses into a particle form when observed or mea-sured. The observer does not create the reality but rather allows a particle form to manifest into an aspect from what was a wave of possibilities. Different actions seem to take place with the same quantum stuff in the presence of different observers, and so individuality is the norm within the oneness of the ambience.

As we saw earlier when we looked at the school of minnows and at the camera alongside the freeway, the most important things to know about a quantum item are its position and its velocity. For an entity in the Newtonian world, you can measure both because they are right out there to be seen. In the subatomic world, things are different. Quantum stuff comes in pairs—for instance, position and momentum—but there is a barrier so that we cannot see or measure the one if we can see or measure the other. If we see its position, we cannot measure its momentum, and if we measure its momentum, we cannot see its position. This is the famous Heisenberg Uncertainty Principle, which holds that if you measure one accurately, you lose knowledge of the other, Thus there is a basic uncertainty about any piece of quantum stuff since only one side of any pair can be seen at once. This uncertainty is also due in great part to the constant changing of energy back and forth between particle and wave forms.

So since unmeasured or unobserved quantum stuff tends to act as waves, but when measured or observed acts as particles, various observers viewing the same wave form will each see it collapse into a different particle form. Just observing quantum stuff changes its character, and scientists feel that the same principles would apply to the big things of our world if they could be measured accurately. We also remember that we deal only with probabilities in the quantum, not specifics. The result is that different truths are experienced by different individuals doing the observing, but everything is part of the one great Truth that is God.

The Role of Variety

This is why there are so many basic religious groups, branches, divisions, and congregations in the world, each with differing rules, rites, and dogmas. Is one right and are all the others wrong? That cannot be, since God is One. Can they all be right? Of course they can. Each fulfills the needs of certain people who are at that particular point in their path of human experience. It should be part of our oneness in God that we see the value in each of the thousands of different groups, since all of them together make up some of the infinity of creation, much as many different tints or shades of different colors make up what looks to be the brown trunk of a tree. It is our job to look at these things from a universal perspective, to pull back and see ourselves as the observers, and to perceive through the spiritual eyes of the Self, rather than be caught up in the specifics by seeing only with the eyes of the ego.

Multiplicity is no problem when seen this way. Let us remember how the quantum introduced the theory of parallel universes that give us the opportunity to live out many different existences at once. This is to our greater fulfillment as well as to our greater happiness by showing that we all are still part of God. It is like a modern novel in which the reader is invited to make a decision about what a character will do at a certain juncture, and then turns to the page indicated by that decision to continue reading. This can happen throughout the book. The next time the reader takes up the book, different decisions might be made, leading to different pages of plot with different outcomes, all existing within the same book at the same time.

This is easier to understand when we reflect that there really is no such thing as time in the totality that is God. Time is a principle allowed to us here so that our linear perspectives can give us a medium for making spiritual decisions. Einstein said that space and time are part of a unified whole, and that the curve of space creates the illusion of time, so that it is not a steady linear progression, but rather a wholeness, an entity, a repetition. This fits our theory just fine. All of our possibilities are a wholeness as part of the infinite creativity of God. And we also remember that time is only the measurement of successive events such that if B comes after A, then there is a lapse between the two events that we call time. But this is only from our limited perspective, Actually, in God there is no time because nothing happens in a linear fashion, so there is no lapse and there is no measurement. Everything just happens simultaneously since the mind of God is in an eternal present with God as the First Is.

This means that each person can attain spiritual growth in a way different from every other person at this particular stage in their experience, and it is of just as much value. In the long run it will be a growth toward oneness with God. Indeed, spiritual growth is a part of the true essence of each person. This leads us to an important realization: no matter how many people are around you as you attend your particular church, synagogue, mosque, pagoda, or assembly hall, spirituality is still an individual thing for you and for each person there. No one is just like anyone else because each is on a personal path. Each brings an individualization of the approximate belief of the group, which is therefore made up of a generality of all the probabilities in attendance. Does that sound vague enough? Well, that is what the situation is like. It is safe to say that no one, not even the leader of the group, is aligned completely and totally with the stated tenets of the organization. Specific spiritual levels are still personal, and yours are just fine.

In fact, since each spiritual leader puts a different spin on the official dogmas within each religious organization, there is not one fixed religious dogma being taught anyway, but only opinions and approximations. This also fits quantum theory, because quantum waves are only measures of probabilities. They cannot be measured accurately, as we have seen, so there are few specific overall facts in the quantum world. Each piece of quantum stuff operates in its own way, somewhat unpredictably (to a great extent because of the Zero Point Field), and can be seen as only a good possibility at best. So you can operate the same way since you are an individualized manifestation of God, finding your own way, yet always a part of the oneness of the whole universe. The variations and possibilities of our individualities are all part of the plan and are to be welcomed since they actually represent unity rather than the separation that the ego would have us see.

What Is EMILY?

EMILY is a compact but thorough way of organizing our efforts to follow our own path. Each step has a different function. The first, Enlightenment, establishes the goal and keeps it steadily before us. We all remember the story of the farmer teaching his son to plow. When the boy complained that he couldn't get the straight rows that his dad did, the farmer explained that the boy had to fix his eye on something distant and go toward it, and this would keep the rows straight. The boy liked the idea, but at the end of the day his rows curved all over the place. When the father was upset about it, the boy said: "Well, I kept my eye on something distant just like you suggested, but the cow kept moving." We need to fix ourselves on one goal that doesn't change, so the first step in EMILY keeps the principle of enlightenment constantly before us as the number one thing at which we are aiming.

And what is enlightenment? It is being aware of God in everyone and everything, and of feeling oneness in the All of the Presence. It is non-duality and is, therefore, the source of true bliss and peace, for when we are in the Presence, nothing more can be needed or imagined as we lose ourselves in Its indefinable joy.

The second step, Meditation, sets the medium through which we work. Meditation is the best method for receiving inspiration and intuition directly from the Source and of becoming aware of the spirituality latent within us that presents itself to us when we turn inward in peaceful contemplation, getting our worldly egos out of the way. Every creative act begins with thought, but we can have thoughts from the self in our brains that chatter away constantly about useless worldly matters, or we can have Thoughts from the Self about spiritual creation, positive relations with others, happiness, and peace. In meditation, we can silence the former and allow the latter to flow as we set the pattern for obtaining enlightenment in our present lives.

The third step, Intention, sets the way we treat ourselves, enlisting the universe to be with us in our journey of self-discovery. Through it, we make a commitment to pursue the goal, thereby allowing spirit to be our companion in the process. There is nothing magical about spirituality: it is there already, merely awaiting our becoming aware of it. When we set our intention to gain this awareness, we find that everything is right there to help us. Things just begin to happen in our favor: certain people appear saying certain things at the right time, opportunities come to us, and the universe just works with the pattern we set.

The fourth step, LOVE (you will see in its chapter why I write it that way), is how we treat everyone and everything in the world around us, although it is also how we need to treat ourselves as part of the process since the person who does not feel the best about himself or herself has a hard time feeling great about others. So in this step we adopt the ways of dealing with ourselves and with others that bring the highest vibrations of consciousness to all of us. In this way we start behaving as if we were enlightened beings already, which is what LOVE really stands for.

The fifth step, Yielding, is how we treat God as well as ourselves and others, and how we facilitate our rise to higher levels of Consciousness by ridding ourselves of all the baggage that is weighing us down. As we yield all to God, we end our identification with worldly agitations, opinions, and uncertainties, entering instead into the peacefulness, stillness, and serenity that mark the Presence and our oneness with It.

So let us consider in detail how EMILY can help us in raising our Consciousness to a higher awareness of and companionship with the Presence. It should be noted that we will look at nothing new since all we need to accomplish our quest is already in us. It just waits to be discovered. As our consciousnesses rise higher and higher, we will see and live great changes that will bring us joy and love and will enrich the lives of those around us, even to the whole world. So therefore EMILY can also mean: EverMore I Love You

Enlightenment

A minister friend of mine always has the congregation repeat with her the basic aims of the church near the beginning of each service so that everyone becomes united with everyone else and focused on the same result because, as she says: "You always begin with the end in mind." Likewise, EMILY starts out with the planned end result so that our minds and our actions remain focused on that realization. Every time we think of EMILY or review the steps in our minds, whether in formal meditation or just informal "course correction" during the day, we first focus on our ultimate goal: Enlightenment.

Discernment

Generally, the word "enlightenment" is used to mean the illumination of our understandings to see new truths. Light symbolizes discernment, the ability to tell one thing from another. There is a chapter in Dumas' novel <u>The Three Muske-teers</u> entitled: "At Night All Cats Are Gray." In the absence of adequate physical light, our eyes cannot discern well, and in the absence of active spiritual receptors, we cannot sense higher Consciousness.

The type of light we use is of great importance. As an example, I can try to sort my socks in artificial light, but my slight colorblindness is such that I can only tell the basic blacks from the basic blues that way. To see the various shades of blue or black among them so that I can match the pairs correctly, I have to go out into the sunlight because of its more complete light spectrum. Girls know that certain artificial light can make their make-up look pasty and turn their lipstick purple. This is because some artificial light is missing colors that are needed to make up true white light, and this can lead to visual errors. A dog uses his nose to discern because his eyes can be fooled. A blind person uses touch, hearing, and a sense of the aura or presence. A wine expert uses taste, since different wines can look the same. So we need a method that encompasses all aspects of reality to help us in our spiritual discernment or enlightenment.

I know several kinesiologists who use the arm test to find truth. A person stands with his or her arm extended straight out from the shoulder. The interviewer makes a statement and immediately presses down on the wrist of the extended stiff arm while the person resists. If the statement is true, the arm remains strong. If is not true, there is a sudden and brief weakness in the muscles and the arm is pushed downward. The theory is that truth is all around us and we have access to it without necessarily being aware of that fact, and so the muscles respond with strength or weakness in response to comments about it. The arm method is covered thoroughly in <u>Power Vs. Force</u> by Dr. David Hawkins. Other people use a method of interlocking the rings made by the thumb and index finger and trying to pull them apart. Others have the person stand erect with eyes closed, and the direction in which they sway, forward or backward, is the answer. Many other muscle tests are used in various ways by kinesiologists testing for disease, back problems, and the like.

We can proceed in much the same manner in our search for spiritual enlightenment. Truth is all around us because God is within all of us, and God is complete at every point, which means that we can receive intuitions directly from the Source when we are able to open our awareness to them. They are all-inclusive, though tailored for us individually, and show the complete natures of things much as the consciousness puts together into one complete picture all the different views of a car that we saw earlier. These intuitions come more easily when we are in the meditative state that will be discussed in the next chapter because it is then that we can calm down some of the mind chatter blocking our awareness of them.

What intuitions are we to discern in our enlightenment? Again, simply the presence of God in ourselves as well as in everyone and everything else, and our total oneness within the Presence. Why should these be individualized and not universal? Because we are on different paths to enlightenment and have different capacities, much as how entering a very bright room from a dark hallway can overly dazzle us temporarily although the light seems normal to those already in the room. Rest assured that God is in charge and all is proceeding correctly. We just need to keep trying to open our awareness to this Presence because of how egos and things of the world constantly set the scene for us to close our eyes to spiritual aspects and remain in darkness.

True enlightenment means an end to duality, that obstacle so very hard just to recognize, much less surpass. Just as non-duality shows us that there is not a God "up there" with us "down here," it also shows that I am not here while you are over there. We are all interconnected as are the electrons that move in unison at great distances in the Zero Point Field. Therefore, we cannot hate or criticize others because they actually are us. This leads to a great feeling of peace because there is nothing to give us agitation. We don't have to be worried or fearful because we know the comfort of God within us. We don't have to find fault or judge or condemn because we are able to yield everything to God, as we will see later. We don't have to carry heavy burdens because they really don't exist. For example, we can look at people going by in a limousine and feel happy that they have what they need for their fulfillment at this point in their existence, rather than feel jealous of their wealth or think we have failed in life because we do not ride in such a vehicle. In true enlightenment, we feel nothing but happiness and complete peace.

Enlightenment in the Prison

Let me give an example. I spent many years as a religious counselor in a state prison. I dealt with people that society had rejected because of the crimes they had committed, spending the majority of my time with rapists and pedophiles, the types of people that even other inmates hate and reject. I went out there determined to see the God presence in every one of them by using a spiritual light that would show them to me as whole and complete, and it worked out just that way. I kept reminding myself that God was in them as well as in me, that they had hopes and fears just like everyone else, and that they were whole and perfect spiritually as I looked at them from my spiritual level of Self. They sensed my acceptance of them and my love for them and they responded. I had many wonderful friends out there. To their credit, many of them achieved a type of enlightenment in which they realized that they had done crimes and had real weaknesses of character that needed to be remedied. Being out of denial about their crimes and being able to see things by a light of empathy for those whom they had offended, many of them did a good job in setting themselves right with God and with society.

Now, to help the inmates acquire the ability to have proper relationships with others, members of churches on the outside were invited from time to time to come out and help out in the regular religious services we held. Some were quite hesitant, of course, and so I would have the group arrive early so I could calm them down and give them a short orientation of how and how not to deal with the inmates, such as not doing favors, not making phone calls for them, not giving out addresses, and so forth. Then I would say: "Now that it is time to start, I would like you to go stand at the door and greet the inmates as they come in so you can get to know them a little better." There was usually a vociferous protest against this because, in their minds, they had only come out to give prayers and a sermon, and they certainly did not want to mix with these people whom they judged to be evil. But I would insist, and so they would agree to it.

Soon the inmates would begin to come in wearing their newest, nicest blue uniforms, all starched and pressed. Their shoes were shiny, their hair was combed, and they smelled good because they were giving respect to God in these services. Hesitantly the visitors would begin to greet them and shake hands, and then two things always happened: the first was that after a while I could hardly stop all the gabbing and visiting to get the services started; the second was that the person giving the sermon would say that the experience of that day had changed the thinking of the group and they now appreciated what these inmates were trying to accomplish in setting themselves aright.

What had happened? My guests had become enlightened as to who these inmates really were and to the realization that God was in them. They now saw that all were whole, complete, and perfect in their spiritual Selves, and were struggling to manifest these characteristics in their earthly personalities and lives. My visitors often commented that they had been led to see what they themselves needed to do to increase their own spirituality.

Let me follow that with a specific story. One of my favorite inmates, whom we will call Jimmy, had been a serious pedophile most of his adult life after having been molested repeatedly as a child as well as forced to do satanic rituals and other damaging things. After many years in prison and with extensive therapy, he was ready for parole, but was scared to go on the outside for fear he might offend again, both for not wanting to hurt anyone else and for not wanting to wind up back in prison for violation of parole. But he went, and what happened a few weeks later is rather amazing.

He was sitting on a bus bench waiting for transportation when he saw a little girl sit down on the bench across the street and a man sit down next to her. Now, one offender knows another, and Jimmy knew what the man was after, but he didn't dare do anything. Soon the girl, obviously nervous, got up and moved to the end of the bench. The man followed and sat down right up against her. Jimmy could take no more. He knew that if he were seen even talking to a child, he could be sent back to prison instantly, but he had a flash of enlightenment. He saw God in the little girl and knew he had to protect her. He also saw the light of God in the predator and felt that he had to be stopped for his own good and the good of society. And he saw the light in himself and knew he had committed so many crimes that this was a chance to pay society back, and if he were re-incarcerated, he would at least have the satisfaction of knowing that he had saved one precious child. This was an enlightenment of true nobility!

He walked across the street, stopping short of the curb and said: "Little girl, are you all right?" "No," she replied in a scared voice. Jimmy asked: "Do you know this man?" She again replied: "No." "Then," said Jimmy to the man, "I will thank you to move away from her." The man stood up and swung at him. That was all Jimmy needed. He was over six feet tall and built to match, so when his many years of frustration went into his return punch, he knocked the man cold. Then he told the girl to run into a shop close by and have them call the police. The man was arrested on the testimony of Jimmy and the girl, and Jimmy himself was given an award!!

Enlightenment Is Within

Enlightenment, then, is the comprehension of the Truth of God. It emerges to our views when we rise above the clutter of egos, both ours and those of other people, and become aware of its existence. It is what is left when all the non-truth is swept away. It is not outside us in some sort of duality, but is sitting within us right now, waiting for us to discover it and enter through it into the peace of God. It is our awareness of the Presence. Complete enlightenment, then, is to recognize and enjoy the totality and peace of God. Partial enlightenment consists of being more or less aware that we are on the pathway toward that goal, feeling the love and joy that precede it. Actually, all of us in our many stages of progress are somewhere on that pathway, but it is the awareness of it that makes the difference. Many people are just not yet cognizant of who they are and where they are on their paths. That is why Enlightenment is put at the beginning of EMILY, for it will keep us aware of our goal every time we review our steps.

And we need to review them often. It is easy to get caught up in the daily routine and forget to put in time toward increasing our awareness of spiritual things. I remember a story from when I was teaching those public relations and salesmanship seminars in the summers. In one portion of the class, I would have a volunteer come up to the microphone and I would ask him or her to talk for one minute on any subject they wanted without saying "um" or "er" or anything like that. These sounds are, of course, just useless delaying words so we can hold the stage while we collect our thoughts. Several volunteers would bravely start out, but would slip up over and over, being required each time to start again. When it was obvious that no one could do it, I would then present a section on overcoming that obstacle.

Well, after one class, a man approached me and could hardly get past all his "ums" and "ers" to tell me that he really had a bad case of this problem. It was quite evident! I saw that he had two little kids with him, so I told him to have the kids follow him around for the whole weekend and every time he said one of those delaying words, he was to pay them a nickel, right on the spot. I cautioned against building up IOU's and paying them off in the evening: it had to be a nickel on the spot, and I advised him to buy several rolls. Two weeks later I was giving a similar class in a nearby town, and he walked up and said: "Dr. Walker, do you remember me?" I was amazed that he could talk so clearly in that short a time. He said that it was the kids: the first day they made over $10! The next day they made only $4, and the third day they stopped following him around because they weren't making any money. The secret? He just had to be reminded over and over not to say those things until this became a habit. (You can understand that, after I had done that segment of the class, I really had to watch my speech habits or the audience would have been all over me!) By the same token, we need to think of EMILY constantly all day, checking ourselves to see if we are achieving our goals, and the E for Enlightenment is right there at the top so that it always remains before us.

Meditation

Meditation has been the subject of seemingly countless classes, articles, chapters, books, and complete courses in our society. I have seen, read of, experienced, and practiced many meditative techniques and have been amazed at the complexity and variety of detail among them. But the central fact is that meditation is still the best way to approach God for one simple reason: God is Peace and Stillness, and being peaceful and still is the only way to sense the Presence. I know there are those who use loud music, pounding rhythms, singing, shouting, dancing, and other athletics to put themselves into a religious trance where they "feel the spirit," as they have told me, These activities are all external, and although God is there with them in these exercises since that is what they need at that point in their development, the true Presence is peaceful, silent, timeless, and seemingly inactive since all creation is there simultaneously. The very experience of finding God in the quantum is an internal process of becoming aware of what already exists as part of us, not an outward manifestation.

It is much like the role of conversation in our society. Since much of our mind chatter consists of rehashing old situations, justifying ourselves, or finding new things to criticize, our conversations with other people tend to be about the same things, and can easily be a waste of effort. Sometimes it is best just to have silence among us and let ourselves communicate on a thought level, enjoying a semblance of the peace of God.

Meditation does try to halt that sort of useless mind chatter and take us into the silence, but it needs to do other things as well. I have developed a method that does many things at once. With all the forms of meditation that I have seen, I have not yet found one that is like it, so it is the one I will show you in this book. It is simple, keeps me focused, and has all sorts of variations to fit my needs at the moment without straying from the simple, central purpose. It has given me amazing results and will do the same for you. What it does is achieve the spiritual mind set that we need in order to accomplish the three remaining aspects of EMILY throughout our lives. It is not just a time spent sitting quietly, which can seem pointless to us because we think we have so much else to do. It actually accomplishes spiritual things. Naturally, you can use whatever method seems right to you, but mine might bear looking into.

Thoughts

As a preparation, let us look again at "thoughts." We are accustomed to having thoughts running constantly through our brains. I understand that researchers tell us we have 60,000 thoughts a day. It often seems as though we have that many per hour as we are surrounded by the complexity of our world, by masses of people with all sorts of needs, and by the many paths that we are trying to follow. Thoughts run chattering through our heads all the time, even when we try to sit down and meditate, and I have seen many methods put forth to control this constant mind noise.

It helps to know that we have very few truly original thoughts each day. As we noted above, most of what runs through our minds consists of old observations, opinions, ego-centered ideas, rehashes of events (and what we should have done better in them), angers, frustrations, justifications, resentments, worries, and even fears. Most of this is just a waste of time. For example, only a tiny fraction of what we worry about ever comes to pass, so we waste a lot of time feeling anxious and nervous, blocking out the beneficial thoughts that could have raised us up instead. We are better off not worrying.

Thoughts of the self are related to our egos and to our relationships with others. We seek to justify ourselves, protect ourselves, look good to others, exercise power and control over others, save face, and a host of other things that have little to do with our oneness with God. Granted, they have something to do with the ways we live our lives in society, but they are not important during our meditations where we seek to identify with God and raise our level of consciousness to a higher spiritual perspective, a level of Consciousness, one that is so strong that we do not need to save face, be afraid, exercise control, or be admired after we leave the meditation room. Our egoistic selves demand that we do these things in the world as marks of our individuality and greatness so that the ego can thrive and control us, but as spirituality increases, the ego diminishes, and when we control the ego, we draw closer to our true Selves.

True meditation, then, is one place where we can leave the ego and its little thoughts to one side and each of us just commune with God through our higher Self. However, the egoistic self will still keep trying to pour its separatist and elitist (or pessimistic and depressing) thoughts through our brains so fast and so constantly that we will have trouble shutting them off long enough to sense the spiritual intuitions we seek from God. This is a situation that must be dealt with.

So, again, what are thoughts anyway? We sometimes consider them to be messages that flow through our brains, but these are only electrical and chemical reactions going through this mass of gray matter in our heads. From where do the original thoughts come? Who is the thinker? The brain receives, processes, organizes, and stores, but does not create, as we already know. And we have seen that much of what the brain does is also done in the cells throughout the body where memory and independent action on the part of the cells duplicate many of the brain's functions. So there must be a bigger definition of "thought" and "thinker" than just the brain.

To see what it is, we have to look at the concept of the thought behind the thought. As we sit in a math class ready to take a test, for example, our surface thoughts may be fixed on reviewing the material. However, the thought behind these thoughts could be one of fear of the unknown (since we don't know what the questions will be), fear of failure, fear of looking bad to everyone else, or even fear of not getting into the college we want because of our bad math grades. But even these just mark a second level of thought. The real thought behind the thought behind the thought, the third level, is that we are not sure of who we are in relation to God, and whether we will get into the heavenly Kingdom or be punished eternally, and therefore this test is terribly important to us since we think our real existence is in this physical plane. We have doubts and concerns about the test because our egos tell us we are weak, fearful, vulnerable beings. Establishing who we really are by changing our thoughts can alter this whole cycle.

What the real thought behind the thought behind the thought *should* be is that we are at complete peace with God. It could include knowing that we will be in the Presence after this earthly learning period is over; that we will learn the things we need to learn on this earth because God is all-powerful; that we have no fear of any suffering because suffering only comes from the ego; and that we feel peace, warmth, and happiness because God is Love and all is right in the long run. What a difference! These are the thoughts of attraction to God that we looked at when we saw the graviton as leading to an acquaintanceship with our multiple dimensions through thoughts. These thoughts are of the Self, our spiritual essence. Therefore, not only may we do better on the exam since fear will not be paralyzing our thinking, but we will have a better perspective on our lives in general regardless of our success in math.

So let us go back to our original question one more time: what is "thought?" This is a question worth pondering. Thought is the action arm of consciousness. A thought is a miniature representation of who we really are, of our true level of vibration. It ultimately represents our attraction either to God or to the world because everything we do or say begins with a thought. The character of our thought collection as a whole indicates our level of consciousness. Do we generally have thoughts of failure, despair, resentment, anger, or being the victim? Or do we generally have thoughts of oneness with others, happiness at the success of others, comfort with who we are, appreciation of the beauty all around us, and acceptance of everyone and everything from our perspective of peace and spiritual contentment? Which type attracts us more to the God within us? Whatever thoughts we dwell on represent the direction in which our consciousness is moving. The old saying is that the true test of people is what they think when they think they are alone. What do we really think? To what are we really attracted?

What Is Needed in Meditation

Remember that thoughts are things and, as such, have both wave and particle identities. In wave form, they represent many aspects and possibilities, and can interact with the wave forms of other people, facilitating the dampening or amplifying of them depending on the correlation. But they still represent potentialities and can range widely without firm attributes. In particle form they become more fixed and lend themselves to definition. Since thoughts precede action, and since as particles they are now in kinetic form, there are no more possibilities. This could be the form used by chi gung and other practitioners in healings and manifestations of power,

And this way of viewing thoughts could be the bridge between two camps of belief about the healing power. One camp says that we may not use willpower in healing, but rather must only become aware of the good health that already exists for the person. Another camp feels that bringing energy to bear on the specific problem brings the power of healing directly to it. Both seem to have great success. How can this be, since they seem to be so different? Well, the first can represent the wave form of thought, and the second the particle form, and both can get results, We just need to remember that neither causes anything, but only sets the scene for the event to occur. The key here is intention, the commitment that turns thoughts into action. Either way, thoughts can travel through our many dimensions and can have effects on us and on others in ways that are not immediately evident in this three-dimensional brane in which we exist.

This can give us a clue as to how we can be of benefit to mankind, even if we are sick in bed or are in prison. Since everything is one, we can spend time generating positive thoughts of love and peace which can set an atmosphere for the whole world, even if just a tiny amount. The cumulative effect of many people joining in such an activity can facilitate a significant rise in consciousness. I remember when some of the women I worked with in prison decided to have group prayer before being locked down for the night. Each evening at 10:45 they would all kneel together in a corner of the dayroom and one would be the voice. It opened the way to great effects in their personal lives as well as in the lives of other inmates and even of the guards, one of whom would key down the intercom from the glassed-in control room and say: "Amen." An important aspect was that they knew that I, their spiritual mentor, was stopping whatever I was doing wherever I was on the outside, and was in prayer with them, the effect uniting us no matter how far apart we might be. It was always a moving spiritual experience.

So just stopping our busy lives of little egoistic thoughts to spend a few minutes sitting quietly will not necessarily improve us much. But using this meditation time to set our intention to one of achieving a higher level of consciousness, or to picture ourselves as moving toward it through spiritual thoughts, or to open ourselves to the flow of intuition from the God within will indeed benefit us. These thoughts are now in particle form. They have life and radiant effects, and they can travel through all our many dimensions. We will see a more complete view of what our thoughts really are in the chapter on Intention.

For now, we need a meditation method that not only sets beneficial surface thoughts, but beneficial thoughts behind the thoughts as well, activating the real thinker that I mentioned earlier. Who is the real thinker? The real thinker is my spiritual Self, the part of me that is in contact with the Presence *unless* I have allowed it to abdicate its position in favor of this ego of mine that is all-too-ready to jump in and control my thoughts from its petty and limited point of view. We all have our self and Self, and we need to be aware of which one is controlling our thinking, the action arm of our consciousness.

How can the ego create and push thoughts that are contrary to those of the Self? Wouldn't God refuse to carry out those thoughts as being contrary to my good? No, this is a part of why we are here in this existence learning the lessons of earth life. We are given the freedom to have an ego and to go through these experiences as part of our development. As we create thoughts within either our selves or our Selves, we emulate the creativity of God since God is part of us. So just as our own subconscious mind carries out the things we plan, the corresponding aspect of the mind of God carries out any thoughts impressed upon it, not just the good ones. Thus we can experience the karma or consequences of these thoughts and our subsequent actions and reactions. This is part of our gaining energy by accelerating upward through the Higgs Field. Earth life would be meaningless if everything were carried out for us by God while we just floated along, regardless of what we might think or want, even at a low level of consciousness. "As a man thinketh, so is he," says the well-known phrase. This is, of course, a great blessing for us, for as we learn to control our thoughts, we are controlling our levels of consciousness and we have the opportunity to be in the Presence when we choose.

Chakras and Visualizing

Before looking at the method I have chosen, we have to understand something of chakras and of visualizing. I am not asking your acceptance of the concept of chakras if it is not to your thinking, nor is it necessary for this meditation. Its reference here is a convenience for explaining the meditation technique, so let us learn what we can for that purpose, if for no other.

For thousands of years, many people have felt that there are special energy centers in the body, places that have greater than normal concentrations of power and flow. The word "chakra" in Sanskrit means "wheels," and is used to refer to certain non-physical centers of life force energy in the body. The seven main ones are the root chakra, based in the sexual organ area at the tip of the spine; the sacral chakra centered in the spleen and liver below the navel; the solar plexis chakra in the stomach area; the heart chakra; the throat chakra; the third eye, centered in the forehead between the eyes and just above them; and the crown chakra at the top of the head. Additional sources of transferable energy are the hands and feet, of course. Other centers have been indicated, but these will do for our purposes. Most of them have functions that are easily seen from their location, but it is important to remember that the root chakra is located in the area of the body from where physical life comes, and so it can be considered as being closely connected with the act of creation. We will refer to chakras during the meditation to aid us in visualizing.

Now for visualization itself. Basically, it is picturing things in the mind. In life, we tend to do this automatically in such situations as looking for something, where we picture the thing we seek in our minds and then, when something we see matches that picture, we focus on it as being what we were seeking. But visualization in meditation is not picturing things as they seem to be in form, but picturing things as they should be with the idea that they *already are* what we see internally. For instance, much of healing treatment consists not of picturing the person as having a disease, but of seeing them as whole, complete, and perfect, and never thinking at all of the disease. Thinking of it is to recognize it and give it life since everything starts with thought. The healer prefers to use thought to give life to a view of the person as whole and healthy, so this is the picture carried in the mind.

Then when people being healed come to accept that picture as being how things really are, they become aware of the internal health and wholeness that they already have as perfect beings created by God, and therefore healing can take place unless their roles in life call for different situations temporarily as part of their development. Awareness of the reality of health is the key. We will treat of this more in the chapter on Intention, but suffice it to say here that in meditation, certain things are pictured in the mind, and the body is allowed to react to them so that there is a completeness and unity throughout the person.

All this is in accordance with the quantum. What we are doing by picturing things as they should be is acting as the observer for whom the wave form collapses into this particular particle form. Note that I do not say that we ourselves collapse the wave, since nothing causes anything in actuality, but we do set the atmosphere for it to become form, and usually health is the form we would wish it to take.

We should note that some meditation methods are unfocused, the aim being to meditate quietly with the mind open to whatever inspiration or intuition might come. Others are focused, concentrating on a single thing that the one meditating prefers to have come to pass. The second is better for stopping the endless mind chatter but the first has more receptivity to allow inspiration to come forth in any area, not just the one concentrated on. Our meditation will be a combination of the two in order to achieve the best of both.

The Method

Now we are ready to begin. We should make ourselves comfortable. Some people sit in a chair, some take various meditative positions, some lie down, some even take the horse stance as in chi gung! Some people like to keep their eyes closed as an aid to concentration, but this is a matter of personal preference. You can meditate just as well either way. You might prefer to have contemplative music playing softly to help silence the mind chatter. Some people like to chant a mantra or sing a hymn to begin, and that is fine. There is something helpful about sounds, especially harmonic ones, or chanting a mantra such as God's name as part of the total vibrations of the meditation. (It is interesting that the Muslims, in their prayers five times a day, only repeat praises to God, with no sermons or complex arguments.) Whatever we do, it is important that we set our intention to open ourselves spiritually so that the intuitions can flow from the Source that is within us.

I often organize my meditation by using the five-point format used by some churches to give order and structure to prayers. I begin by affirming that there is only One: one Power, one Creativity, one Source for all the energy, life, and intelligence that exist anywhere, and that One is God. The exact words are not important. What is important is for me to set my conviction that God is omnipotent so that there is no obstacle in my thinking to the flow of God's creative intuition. I show that I do not believe in any power that can thwart it. Then in the next step I affirm my unity with that One, stating my conviction that I am one with God and that I am vibrating on my higher spiritual frequencies in harmony with my Source. Then, with my sensitivities opened, I move into the step of visualizations, which I will discuss in a moment. After this, I give thanks for the meditation, for the inspirations I have received, and for the awareness that has let me uncover more and more of the fulfillment that is within my Self all along. I then release or yield everything to God to be carried out in the way that is of the greatest benefit to all. This way I do not distract or obstruct the flow of spirit by trying to hang in there and do things my way anyhow. Releasing also keeps me peaceful because I don't have to fret about the outcome. I just relinquish everything, letting it be, and emerge from the meditation refreshed and spiritually more aware.

This method can also be used for actual prayer since prayer, as we have seen, is not a plea to some external deity but an opened awareness to God as being within and a knowledge that all things for our good are already present, only needing to be recognized to manifest in our lives. The five steps can be followed in such a prayer and ended with: "And so it is," which is the same as: "Amen."

The third step is the complex one. I do a variety of things and will present them here in no particular order. One is that I imagine a flow of energy going through my body from the root chakra, the creative area, up to my third eye area through which I visualize something desired, such as the good health of someone who is ill, or success in some undertaking of mine. As I carry the picture of that situation as done and complete, I tie that image back into my root chakra to show it as now being created that way,

Note that I do not create the form that such success will take; I leave that up to God. If I insist on having it happen just my way, I am not only showing distrust in God, but also am limiting myself since God has many more ways to accomplish things than I am aware of. If I were to picture a better job for myself, for example, I should not picture getting a particular one that I have in mind, but rather should just picture myself as happy and working and earning what I need. The actual job that shows up may be something completely different from what I would have imagined.

I sometimes picture a similar flow of energy from the root chakra to the throat chakra if I am going to counsel someone or give a talk to a group or even perform musically. I picture and accept the idea that my success in that endeavor is already an accomplished fact. I envision the same flow to the heart to enable me to be more sensitive to others and willing to give myself in loving service to them. I even image such a flow to my hands if I am going to lay hands on someone for a healing treatment or go do a job for someone, and I see the proper energy as flowing profusely.

On the other hand, I will also picture a flow from my crown chakra, the symbolic place of receptivity of intuition, back to these areas, showing my acceptance of inspiration and intuition in the carrying out of my endeavors. Of course, all knowledge is already in me since God is in me and I just need to open my awareness to be able to effect it, but opening the crown chakra symbolizes the flow of such thoughts or awareness inward from the totality of the Universe and its knowledge as well as from within going outward, and can focus my attention on the flow itself. And I picture the incoming flow as spreading from the crown throughout the body as I feel enlightenment fill my being. In this I am actually opening myself to God, to inspiration, and to healing, and I can feel the affected parts getting warmer.

I also picture energies flowing from my various chakras to the crown chakra and out into the universe. Sometimes this is to image my releasing all things to God, even though God is within. Sometimes it means releasing them to the world for the benefit of all. Since we are all one on this earth and in the Universe, any high-vibration energy that I release raises the energy levels of the whole world, no matter how tiny the amount, as we saw before. A good time to do this is just after reading the newspaper or listening to a news broadcast: instead of being upset at the news, I can meditate on loving and healing truth for the affected peoples. Slowly, slowly the world is evolving to higher levels, and part of that is due to those people with very high levels of Consciousness concentrating on an awareness of Good for everybody. We remember that thoughts are the activity arm of consciousness, and the higher the thoughts, the higher the level of consciousness. Lower levels of consciousness involve such destructive illusions as jealousy, guilt, anger, and the like, whereas the highest levels involve unconditional love, forgiveness, and all the things that we will look at in the next chapters. Picturing these as radiating through the head chakra is a good way to do our part for humankind, for the earth itself, and for the universe.

A key point in all of this is that I must maintain my identity as Self and be cognizant of my awareness at all times. I do this by pulling back, even seeming to rise above my body, in order to see myself doing these things. I have to see myself as the observer functioning from a heightened level of consciousness because that way I am more at the level of my Self, rather than remaining locked into the ego aspects of the self. I have to see the oneness of all things and the light of Consciousness in everything so that I can remain open to the oneness of the Presence.

As you can see, this method combines the open-minded receptivity of one kind of meditation with the focused style of another. It has plenty of variety going on to block the idle and useless chatter of the unruly, lower-level thoughts of the brain that we usually have a tough time controlling, but also allows the quiet and peace needed to receive intuition and to empty the mind so proper thoughts can be attracted in.

Finally in this middle section of the meditation, I review each element in EMILY, focusing first on my commitment to achieve the enlightenment that I seek, then focusing on the meditation as my preparation to receive this enlightenment, and finally reviewing the three steps to keep them planted firmly in my consciousness and operating in my life.

Since it is my intention that opens the way to the flow, let us now look more closely at that concept.

Intention

When I was housefather to a set of teenage abused boys some years ago, one of them was in a karate class and had a test coming up: he was to break a board held by his instructor by a kick with his bare foot. He was concerned about wanting to doing well on the test without hurting his foot, so he resolved to do the assignment by kicking at the board and hoping for the best. This mindset, of course, was a recipe for disaster because his intentions were all wrong.

Why? To answer that we have to look at what is meant by the word "Intention." Usually, it is thought of as a plan or a goal to accomplish something, coupled with a strength or focus on actually getting it done. The tricky part is that, since we are of God and God is in us, our thoughts and plans become part of the Mind of God that subsequently carries them out. So intention is not just an idea flitting through our brain but is part of the vast storehouse of creative energy that is God, as represented by the huge Field seen earlier that is involved in the creation of everything that exists. We recall that there is room in the infinite creativity of God for all things to be carried out whether or not they are for our immediate betterment, because that is one of the values of this human experience and is our chance to witness the results of our thoughts and actions as part of our growth process. If I imagine fears or lacks, they will tend to manifest in my experience. If I imagine positives and plenty, they will tend to manifest. It is like staring at something to the side when we are driving a car: we tend to swerve toward it. This is all part of the infinite nature of God.

Positive Intention

I well remember one of the first times I stood with a fellow professor of mine on the #10 tee of Dos Lagos Golf Course near the University of Texas at El Paso where we both taught. Our tee shots had to clear a broad lake before hitting the fairway. In his comments on the size of the lake and how hard it would be to cross it, my friend was unconsciously setting an intent to fall short of the fairway and put his ball in the water, which he promptly did, saying afterward that his swing just didn't feel right. I set my intention on hitting the fairway beyond the lake and seeing my ball rolling far down it. Well, my tee shot wasn't much better than his and my ball also hit the water, but my intention allowed me to hit it so hard that it had enough force and top spin to skip six times along the surface of the water, jump out, and roll fifty yards down the fairway! Intention is part and parcel of accomplishment, and what we accomplish depends greatly on the intent with which we approach it.

So let us see what part intention was playing with my boy in the karate class. In the first place, he was dwelling on the desire of not getting hurt, so this is where some of his intention lay. However, the mind does not understand negatives too well, so when we picture not getting hurt, the mind focuses on the "getting hurt" part. I remember Doc Bulkley, my old colleague at UTPB, who would take visitors to the golf course there in Odessa, Texas, and on the fifth hole carefully point out that it was out of bounds to the right. He would explain that there were open fields to the right, and any ball hit to the right would be out of bounds, so in the tee box they were not to hit to the right, nor were they to hit to the right when on the fairway. All the way to the green they were to remember not to hit to the right. His underhanded strategy worked every time. Even people who had not hit a slice in their whole lives saw their ball zoom into a big curve off to the right and disappear while Kent appeared to feel so sad about it because he had tried to warn them. The trick was, of course, that he never mentioned the word "left;" he only used the word "right" as a caution not to go there. As I said, the brain does not always hear negatives. Therefore the word that was implanted in the minds of his victims was the word "right," so they invariably went there, and he cheerfully picked up their stroke and distance. Knowing that story, I knew that my boy was on the road to hurting himself since "hurt" was the word on which he was putting his intention.

In the second place, his goal was to do only what he was asked, so the idea of backing off a little and doing the least possible was implanted. In the third place, he intended not to look bad to everyone, so the idea "looking bad" was formed in his intention regardless of the negative he tried to put on it. In the fourth place, he was focused only on the board, and therefore his foot would have the intention to stop there, which means that it would not have the follow-through to actually break it.

To appreciate what happened next, we need to stop here and consider the wave-particle aspects of thoughts once again. We measure brain waves with an EEG but we look at the electro-chemical reactions in our brains as things, so which are we in this physical life? The quantum has already told us the answer: we are both. Our thoughts can be waves when they are full of potential, spreading out all over as they test the different ramifications of various possibilities, and then they are particles when specific paths are decided upon. This helps us realize that random thoughts of suicide or an affair should not fill us with guilt or lesser self-images, but should rather be seen as various potentialities available to us. What we specifically decide upon, what the wave form collapses into, is more the measure of our character and spirituality at this moment because the wave form is more our basic overall essence as it carries all of our possibilities.

It is interesting that we speak of enlightenment using the effect of the little photon, light, as a symbol of our increased awareness of God in everything. In the same way, if the graviton is related to thoughts, we need to see its role as an attractor, something that draws things (or allows them to be pushed) together. Our thought waves are potentiality, but our thoughts in particle form are those to which we are really attracted, the ones that lead us to actions in our lives. We can go back to the golf story in which we see that the brain does not recognize the negative, so that if we try to think of not slicing the ball to the right, it will promptly sail off in that direction. By the same token, if we spend a lot of time thinking of or hearing about things we should not do, such as various acts labeled "sins" in the codes of different religions, we are actually spending time thinking about them and being attracted to them because they are so much on our minds, and we therefore may wind up doing them!

This is like a church organization I know about that will not let a man and a woman ride alone together in a car even if they are church leaders going out on ecclesiastical business. This may be meant to avoid any possible sinful behavior, but the message is hammered on so often that the constant emphasis only keeps the idea to mind since the mind does not recognize negatives! So if such leaders ever do get into a car, even with others and even though both are happily married, just the act of getting close like that reminds them of the possibility, and they feel guilt along with a little fear until the ride is over.

You might try this little exercise: make yourself sit in a corner quietly somewhere for half an hour and not think of a glass of water. You will soon see that the act of being there in the corner and knowing why you are spending some of your time there will constantly bring the water to your mind. You may think of other things for a while, but then you might check your watch and marvel that it has been ten minutes already that you have sat there and not thought of...oops, you just did and now you have to start all over. You may even develop a thirst just from not being allowed to think of the water, which will make it even more diffi-cult. The only way to do it is to forget all about the time and just concentrate your mind completely on another line of thinking. Filling your mind totally with positive thoughts gives the ego little chance to allow mental glimpses of the water glass to slip through.

In real life, what happens is that the act of keeping ourselves concentrating totally on higher concepts affects our thoughts behind the thoughts behind the thoughts, those of the Self, and thus our spiritual nature overrides the ego and its little earthly naggings, temptations, or thoughts of petty satisfaction of lower desires. Real Intention takes over, and our spiritual Self is seen in its rightful place as the center of our being. So I gave this boy some advice: set your high-level Intention to remain whole, complete, and perfect in body, enjoying a growing experience in this activity, and then set your regular intention only on driving through the board to hit your instructor with your foot. Think of nothing else. Why does a needle go through a cloth? Because its force is concentrated on a tiny point. Pushing your finger against the cloth just spreads the force over a wide area and it won't go through. I pointed out to the boy that he had trained and condi-tioned his body and feet, and that the instructor would not have him do some-thing that could actually allow harm, so there was nothing else to think about. Actually, he would hurt himself less against a board that broke away from his foot than against one that stayed firm as his foot smashed against it. And concentrat-ing on driving through the board all the way to the instructor would supply the follow-through necessary to accomplish the task completely. Then I went with him to the dojo so he would know to remember the things I had said. The board, of course, was shattered and the foot was fine.

It is useful to think of intent and Intent just as we think of self and Self. Both intent and Intent are of God and are beneficial to us in the long run as they both take place, but the former refers to the ego-based, material world experience while the latter refers to the Self-based, spiritual oneness with the Presence. The latter is the real thought behind the thought, and if it is well in place, the former will tend to reflect it in a higher level of Consciousness.

Intention and Focus

So it is with us when we consider EMILY. Once we have decided on our goal of enlightenment, and once we have prepared ourselves through meditation, we have to go forth with the intention to accomplish what we have planned. We need to be single-minded about this and keep our intentions at the same high level. Once we set ourselves on the course, all else will fall into place as we follow our original plan, but if we split our intentions, we can wander all over and accomplish very little. Nothing can make us swerve from the path to our goal except ourselves, so constant focus is necessary, and we can remind ourselves of this every time we think of EMILY.

Let us see this in a practical way. When I was teaching religion in a high school, we were given the story of a railroad engineer who was running his passenger train at its normal high speed and rounded a corner only to see in front of him the wreck of a freight train that had jumped the tracks. Most of the cars were off to the side, but two were sticking out partially over the track. He had only a couple of seconds to decide what to do. Without hesitation, he gunned it! His train hurtled down that track with all the speed he could muster and he hit those freight cars so hard he knocked them out of the way and his train remained upright on the track with his passengers safe. Hitting them more slowly while trying to stop would have let their inertia derail him. When asked later how he had the presence of mind to make such a great decision, he replied that long ago he had set his Intention [my capital letter] to be a good, safe engineer, and therefore had gone over in his mind the things he could do when faced with each of the many situations that can occur while a train operates. He made a carefully thought-out decision about every one of them so that all those intentions were in place ahead of time, and were kept in place by his original Intention [again, my capital] of being a safe engineer. Thus it was that, when faced with this particular situation, he did not have to think. He followed his original plan and came out fine.

We can do the same. We can set our spiritual Intention and not have to worry about fiddling with it or changing it to fit new situations. When we are dealing with something as important as enlightenment and our level of Consciousness, we just change the situation to fit our Intention and we come out just fine. In my talks I refer to it as commitment. We commit to follow a certain path toward uncovering our own enlightenment by doing the elements in EMILY. By that commitment, we set the Intention. Without commitment, any intention is only a wish.

Intention Is Power

Real intention with commitment is power, an existing strength that we can tap into, and we do it all the time. This needs to be emphasized. All thoughts are in the Mind of God, so any intention we have, whether for our betterment or for our detriment, is put into motion by this Mind, as we have seen before. We have to be careful about our thoughts, for the intentions in them will become part of the Field, set to come to pass. Also, we don't create intention out of nothing any more than we create enlightenment out of nothing. These things already exist and we just uncover or become aware of them. Intention is a power, not a force. It does not push its way around, using up energy, and creating its own back-lashes. It just sits there immoveable, giving energy and fulfillment when we adopt it as ours.

As an example of that, I well remember being a teaching assistant at UCLA in the late sixties when mobs of students protesting the actions of the establishment were rioting on college campuses all over the country, taking over administrative offices, and creating fear everywhere. UCLA had its share of these problems and I often watched as police and demonstrators clashed openly. One day as I was teaching an undergraduate class, the moment widely feared by professors arrived: three wild-looking students burst into my classroom and announced that they were taking over the class to denounce the hated establishment. I had set my Intention long ago, and so I replied firmly that they were going to sit down and shut up. That got their attention. I told them in no uncertain terms that I was in charge of the class, not they, and that I was going to finish my work there. I then added that, as a courtesy to them, I would finish five minutes early and they could have the rest of the time if anyone cared to stay and listen to them, but in the meantime they were to back off and sit down. They did so and waited quietly the rest of the class. Why? Because I had the power of Intention on my side. They weren't really sure of themselves but I was very sure of myself and my power was visible. I ended my lesson early and left, and had no more trouble with student activists the rest of my time at UCLA.

Now, what was my Intention? Maintaining control of the situation in the classroom was only a ramification of it. Staying safe was not it because I was actually courting disaster by my stance. No, there was a deeper motive. I was an independent, freedom-loving citizen of an independent, freedom-loving nation (does my being born on the Fourth of July have something to do with it?) and I did not want to see myself or my country give in to unruly mobs intent on tearing us down. Their right to protest, which was fine, did not include the right to intrude on my peacefulness in this instance, to my thinking. (You will recall the fist and the nose syndrome.) This commitment was well in place long before the incident, and when push came to shove, I followed my basic Intention without even thinking about it just as the engineer did. My reaction was automatic, and the power was behind me. Both the intruders and the class felt it, and when I walked out, most of the students went with me.

Understanding Intentions

Which leads us to consideration of the ego and the understanding of true intentions. When I was running those salesmanship classes back in the sixties, I would stay for several weeks in the community I had chosen for the class, visiting all the businesspeople in town, selling them the idea of the class, and enrolling their employees in it. I cannot forget one clothing store I went into where, while waiting to talk to the manager, I watched a clerk trying to get a man to buy a coat. I say "clerk" because he certainly was no "salesman." He just ran back and forth bringing coat after coat, being rejected by the customer each time. Obviously, he did not know the actual need of the customer, and certainly not his real intention. I decided that this wasn't doing the customer any good, so I approached and said: "That's a beautiful coat you have there, neighbor." "I don't like it," he grumbled, "it's too hot." Now, this was in the days of the new, colorful double-knits and they were indeed warmer than conventional fabrics. But an old sales adage holds that a man has two reasons for doing something: one that he will tell you, and the real one. This man had just told me the first and I had to get to the second, so I used the old "Yes, and...." technique by saying: "Yes, and what else bothers you about the coat?" I had given credence to the first one and now I was just going around it. "Aw," he said, "it makes me look like a peacock!"

Now I had something I could work with. The colors were the real issue. His short-term intent was not to look foolish, but his bigger Intent was to be successful and to look it by wearing these success-oriented fashions. This was obvious because he was there in the store looking at the new clothes in the first place. He *wanted* to look good by wearing those styles, and just needed to be told it was

OK. "That is what is so great about these fashions," I said, dressed in the latest myself. "They are new and colorful. They are what is happening right now. When you walk down the street in these beautiful clothes, people are going to say: 'There goes a man of the times, who is with it and in step, successful, looking good because he is part of today's scene.' You will have confidence in yourself, the admiration of others, and the knowledge that looking like the image of success will lead you to being an actual success in whatever you do." Did I sell him the coat? Of course! I also sold him double-knit pants, a striped shirt, a tie and a belt! I understood his true Intention, (Maybe his intention included having me show up!) The astonished clerk wrote up the order and that man went out of there in a happy, positive frame of mind with his real goals fulfilled. What is funny is that the store owner still would not put any of his employees into my class. Oh, well.

When we set any intention, we set in motion the power of the universe to allow that thing to happen through collapse of the wave form. We need to keep aware of what our real Intentions are and not let our egos keep feeling lesser, earth-bound desires, since what we think about, comes about, as we said earlier. This is a vital step in uncovering our true awareness and spirituality. Meditation is a good time to do this. We can meditate on what really helps us feel good, what really brings us satisfaction, what will most raise our level of consciousness toward our goal of enlightenment, and then picture it in the chakras. When we then set our intentions to accomplish it, we just go out and live our plan so that the universe can allow it to come to fruition.

So take time to examine yourself, your real motives, your real needs, your real goals, then set your intentions to accomplish these and commit yourself to stick to them. As a famous frontiersman in America said: "Be sure you're right, then go ahead." When we do that, the power behind intention kicks in and things flow for us. This is why there are so many stories of miracle healings in all kinds of churches under different circumstances and in varieties of ways. It is because there is a power of intention that is common to all. It is interesting that, in the accounts of healings by Jesus, every person had to do something, such as take up their bed and walk. When they rose to do that, showing their power of intention, that power itself was part of the healing process. If they had stayed lying there doubting that it could be done, the infirmity would have continued because that would have been their intention. We all have purposes and they all get carried out. It is up to us to be sure they are the right and proper intentions for our greatest good and the greatest good of everyone and everything around us.

Now we are ready to carry out the action step of EMILY in which we relate to others. It is a big one.

LOVE

This word is understood on so many levels by so many different people who are on such distinct paths that I have hesitated to use it. I feel that these levels are so firmly implanted in my good readers that most would have trouble recognizing a new definition. The concept of romantic love, for example, runs the gamut from the bucolic love of shepherds and shepherdesses who never really get together in their elysian fields, to a rough inflamed encounter of near strangers in a hotel, and from the excitement of first love between adolescents to the warm, quiet, and steady love through the years of a faithful husband and wife. Also, romantic love is still so subject to angers, possessiveness, and downright selfishness that it hardly qualifies as a means to enlightenment anyway. Readers of the Bible point to the various types of love pictured there from filial to agape, and this is on the right track. But even with that, the commonly accepted views that the word "love" brings to mind run through such a range of stages and definitions that there is no way to pin the word down to one specific definition that we can use here. If I use the word, I cannot be sure just what images or feelings will come to the minds of the readers, and these images will tend to color what comes next.

And it is also clear that love, being subject to strong passion, is an emotion, and many such emotions are too fleeting, variable, and subject to mood swings to be permanent parts of our enlightenment unless accepted as principle, as we saw earlier. So let us consider a definition that can serve as a principle, a steady guide that is not subject to mood swings or misinterpretations regardless of what may happen. To do this, I will take the unusual action of using love as the title of this step without referring to it at all!

What is LOVE?

Instead, let us use it as an acronym for the phrase: "Level Of Veritable Enlightenment." The word "veritable," of course, means "real" or "genuine." By doing the things in this chapter, we will be behaving as if we were already enlightened in this earthly existence. This is not a case of "fake it 'till you make it" because the behaviors outlined here are the outward characteristics of someone who has indeed achieved inner enlightenment, and so we are already participating in the higher levels of relationships that mark this state. It is a beautiful way to live, both for us and for the others with whom we relate or to whom we release our healing energies.

Basically this LOVE consists of treating everyone and everything, including ourselves, with constant kindness, forgiveness, compassion, acceptance, caring, appreciation, honesty, generosity, patience, tolerance, peacefulness, thoughtfulness, unselfishness, and all the other high-level attributes of the Consciousness that you can think of. Moreover, this should be done all the time, every day, no matter what others do or how we feel. It should be done with children, animals, and the earth itself. It should not be something done as a chore, but rather should become one's way of life insofar as possible. We all have our weaknesses, I included, so perfection may not be likely, but this is where intention keeps things going for us: we just forgive ourselves if we slip, and go right on.

Is that list too long and daunting? We will reduce it drastically in a moment.

Does the ego suffer when we deal in LOVE? Of course it does, and that is a good thing. We know that the ego advocates separatism and superiority, characteristics that get in the way of our discovery of enlightenment. By dealing in LOVE, we end the idea of separation and give people a new set of higher ideas of who we are and of who they are in our eyes. It is good for us and for others when we form new opinions, and now is the best time to do it.

Jerry and LOVE

Let me tell you a story about that. When I was teaching religion at the high school level, I had a sophomore student whom I will call Jerry transfer into my class mid-year. He was known to run with a rough crowd, so the other students in the class didn't have much to do with him at first, and he reinforced this by sitting apart and keeping to himself. But I felt that he had a lot to offer (and that my students had a lot to learn about reaching out to others), and so I began asking him the typical questions of a lesson as I went along. He always had the answer and was obviously quite bright. I praised him a lot in front of the others and they began to appreciate him more. I made him a zone leader and he led his zone well in all the activities of the class, seeming to enter a new phase of life.

Naturally, I talked a lot in class about our really living our religion and treating everyone with kindness, forgiveness, acceptance, and respect. I also talked about living to our highest selves and having good self-esteem because we are all God's manifestations and, as such, are all of great worth. I urged the students not to pay attention to the criticisms of others because those criticisms have nothing at all to do with them; they only have to do with the complainers and their need to find fault, as we saw in the first chapter of this book. I suggested that they should be positive, helpful, and caring toward others instead, living a life of enlightenment as a big step toward actually achieving it.

Jerry apparently listened well to what I was saying because he came to me at the end of the school year to announce that he had decided to change his life and all of his friends. He admitted that he had been running with the wrong crowd because he felt that they were the only ones who would accept him. After thinking about what we were saying in class, he realized that he needed to have more feelings of self-worth, more confidence in himself, and more desire to reach out and treat others in positive, uplifting ways, being interested in them and helping them succeed. So he had set his intention to take that first big step of changing all his friends. I congratulated him, and waited all summer to see how this worked out.

As classes began again in the fall, I ran into him and asked about the situation. He had indeed done it, and when he told me the list of people he was close to now I was amazed because they were the movers and shakers of the school. He had just forgotten himself and had begun to give service to everyone. As a result, he grew steadily in popularity all year and was even elected King of the Junior Prom. Then when he announced at the end of the year that he was running for Men's Association President, he was so popular that no one would file against him, even though all the other offices had many contenders each. He was a powerful president, and when he got up in front of the student body and did his imitation of the Principal, the Principal and I standing together in the back of the room almost fell down laughing because he was so good at it. He created a whole new persona for himself and we can do it too.

I promised earlier that I would cut my list down to a manageable amount, so let's do it. I suggest that we take just the first two of those characteristics and dwell on them. I feel that they cover all the rest, while being easy to remember and use. They are: kindness and forgiveness. Let us make them firmly entrenched principles in our lives.

Kindness

Kindness involves many things: enjoying and appreciating others; dealing gently with them; speaking softly and pleasantly to them; feeling empathy for them; being courteous, benevolent, honest, and of one mind with them; identifying with their situations; thinking good, positive thoughts about them while outwardly giving real compliments and encouragement; assisting them in what they are doing; helping them feel liked and appreciated; raising their self-esteem; being there when they need to talk but never repeating to others what they say; seeing good in them and learning to understand them better; being someone they can count on; treating them as we would want to be treated; and so forth. (Does the Golden Rule come to mind? No, not the one that says: "He who has the gold, rules." The other one.) Kindness is actually a way of constantly regarding other people (and ourselves) in pleasant and positive ways, a method of continually showing a pleased acceptance of them. Of course, it helps us feel good too, and serves as a role model to onlookers who may then tend to follow suit, and so the wave influence spreads.

Kindness, then, is a high-level, happy way to live life and to regard others. If salespeople are curt or rude, a few kindly words to them may reveal that they are trying to cope with serious problems, and when we understand this, we can show the warmth and empathy that they may need at the moment. When family members snap at us, we just realize that they are battling some frustration, and we reply with compassion. When we see someone sitting alone in church or at a meeting, we reach out and take them into our circle. We donate to the person on the street who asks for a little help. Kindness consists of seeing the God nature in everyone through our spiritual eyes, and therefore is a big part of enlightenment itself.

Of course, we need to show this same kindness to ourselves. We need to treat ourselves well, think highly of ourselves, and encourage ourselves to do good, uplifting things. And we need to be kind to the un-met people of the world through sending out positive prayer affirmations when we hear of their troubles. I often walk down the street picturing the people I meet as being surrounded by the white light of purity and discernment, and I wish them a happy life. Animals instinctively like the person who is kind, as do children, so a kind person spreads warmth and good will wherever he or she goes.

It isn't easy to do, of course, We are often under pressures at work or at home or from financial difficulties, and we often don't feel too patient or tolerant with others, especially family members. We actually need to bless family members and those who tend to bring out the worst in us because they are our best teachers, showing us where we have yet to improve. I remember the true story of two commuters getting off the train from New York one evening. One of them bought his usual evening newspaper from a vendor who just snarled at him when he tried a pleasant remark. As they walked away his friend commented on the vendor's bad humor. "Oh, he's always like that," replied the man. His friend was amazed. "Then why do you let him talk to you that way? Why don't you tell him off?" The man replied: "Why should I let his attitude disturb my peace of mind?" Maintaining a kindly peace of mind and passing it on to others, including snarling vendors, is one of the marks of an enlightened person.

Forgiveness

Hand in glove with kindness is forgiveness. Now, there should not be much forgiveness needed if we are kind, because we will not take things so personally in the first place that we have to go to the step of forgiveness at all. The truly kind person does not have lesser feelings toward others, but yet we are all human and there are times when we feel offended or betrayed, so forgiveness is vital. It just means to release whatever lesser feelings we have and give them up completely while thinking well of the other person. It does not mean to pardon, which would mean that there really was a breach to be dealt with in the first place. We recall that no one can make us less happy; we make ourselves less happy. If we have taken something wrong, that is usually just of our own doing, so there really is nothing for which to pardon the other person anyway.

Forgiveness should be ongoing and constant, with no thought of retribution, vengeance, or punishment for the perceived misdeed. Actually, it involves just forgetting the source of our lesser feelings since continually thinking of them gives them sustained life. We have to remember that we see things only through our limited perspective, and so we may be imagining an affront where there is none, or we may be ignorant of this person's background and ways of doing things in general. It is best just to let things go and clear our minds of them.

Forgiveness is for our own benefit, not that of the other person. They may not care whether we forgive them or not, and may not even know that they have offended us. Our forgiveness is to cleanse ourselves inside by getting rid of destructive feelings so that the higher vibrations of enlightenment can take place in us unhindered. Forgiveness should be instantaneous, not coming after some prolonged mental struggle in which we imagine ourselves the aggrieved person or the innocent victim or anything else that is purely a matter of ego. Some people seem to like feeling put upon, and appear to spend a lot of time letting thoughts of vengeance or retribution flow through their minds, the type of thought chatter that we should try to put aside in our meditations, as we pointed out earlier. If we forgive instantly, we cut down on the chatter, thus giving our egos less to do. They then tend to waste away, thereby allowing the Self to be paramount.

How often do we forgive? Bible readers know well the story of when Peter came to the Christ and posed that question, asking if it should be seven times. Christ responded that it should be seventy times seven. Now, the trick here is that the Hebrew writers used many symbols in their writings, some of them being numbers. "Seven," being a prime number, shared with "three" the idea of perfection and completeness, but added the idea of infinity. So Peter was really asking if we should forgive our enemy an infinite number of times. Jesus' reply indicated that it should be an infinite multiplied by an infinite and even that times ten! This is a different answer than the Western mind is used to. It means that we should always forgive. Always, always. Actually, we should not have any enemies in the first place. There may be people who don't like us for one reason or another, but if we can't clear it up with them, we just forgive and go on our way without a thought about it. How they feel about us is their business and has nothing to do with us at all. We will treat them kindly whenever we see them, and their response to that is also their own decision. No one manipulates us with their bad feelings because our feelings are our own concern and we keep them uplifted.

What is felt for others when using LOVE is a steady, dependable, caring type of good will, always present, accepting, encouraging, and seeking the best for everyone. This is a difficult concept to put across when people are accustomed to thinking of love as romance and passion, but when seen as the acronym LOVE, the different meaning comes through. So let us use kindness and forgiveness with everyone as our Level Of Veritable Enlightenment, and remind ourselves of this

LOVE every time we consider EMILY and what is truly important to us in our present existence.

Yielding

This chapter is very short, as a symbol of what it is saying. The fifth step in EMILY is to yield everything to God. This means giving up any thought of making judgments or criticisms of other people, or of enjoying low-vibration feelings about them. It means releasing everything to God instead, knowing that it all works out for the best. And this needs to be started right now. Short and simple, just like this chapter.

Things that we need to yield include such illusions as vengeances, jealousies, affronts, prejudices, superiorities, irritations, envies, prides, angers, miseries, and so forth. We must give up feeling indignant or slighted or dumped on or made the innocent victim. These are all actions of the ego, which gets its pleasure from our hurt feelings. None of this can exist when we achieve our awareness of the Presence.

These lower concepts are based on the earthly idea that other people can make us feel less happy, angry, betrayed, put upon, verbally abused, or any of the other destructive emotions on which the ego feeds to sustain itself, or on the equally lower-level idea that we are justified in blaming others when we have these feelings. We now know that we alone are responsible for our reactions and emotions, and therefore we have the power to keep them on a high plane. For example, if we are driving down the freeway and a car cuts in front of us causing us to slam on our brakes to avoid hitting it, we can react with rage and retaliation, or we can ignore the situation and continue our conversation. It is up to us. The driver cannot make us angry; only we can open ourselves to being angry, and it is our decision. We can react to all kinds of supposed affronts with fury or with forgiveness; it is our choice. Through the power of instant forgiveness, most events will not be taken as affronts in the first place.

As to personal relationships, we can either love some idealized vision of another person and be full of judgments and criticisms when they do not live up to this ideal, or we can accept and love them with kindness and forgiveness just as they are. Again, it is our choice.

How do we know when we are having success in this last step? The test is simple: our thoughts are uplifted. We keep good thoughts of others rather than catch ourselves rehashing in our mind all the ways they have treated us badly. We see them in a consistently good light. We look for the best in them and in ourselves, and rejoice when we find it. In fact, we are cheerful most of the time, for we let nothing bring us down. Our egos have little to do.

When we begin to curb these egos, preventing them from representing us, and instead yield everything to God, then we discover more and more of our true values, which are spiritual and are in the Self. As the ego keeps diminishing in importance to us, the peace of the Presence keeps growing in our awareness. Then we feel warmth, love, stillness, oneness, and awareness of being filled with the peace of God. Our joy is full.

And this is what is meant by Finding God in the Quantum.

978-0-595-39985-7
0-595-39985-1

Printed in the United States
65981LVS00005B/412-435

9 780595 399857